The Empathy Deficit

How Small Acts of Care Can Restore Unity in a Divided Society

Laura Caruso

Finesse Books

Photography: Alexandra Kelly Photography, https://www.akelly.photography/

ISBN: 978-1-917496-06-3

First edition 2025 published by Finesse Books

FINESSE
BOOKS

Contents

To my parents —

*For choosing to evolve when staying
the same would've been easier. Our relationship
is evidence that healing is possible.*

Introduction

Most people fear death because they dread the unknown of what comes after. I fear death because I'm terrified of not living. Despite the chaos and uncertainty of today's world, it's the small, everyday moments that shape my perspective. It's in these brief interactions—shared smiles, acts of kindness, and quiet reflections—that I find meaning and connection.

In recent years, the fear of the unknown has taken on new forms, sinking its weight into everyday life. Many of us have come of age during a time of upheaval marked by political instability, social unrest, and isolation. From dog-whistle politics, a global refugee crisis, and the rapid spread of a virus that forced 3.9 billion people across ninety countries and territories into lockdown, each new headline only reinforces this uncertainty. This relentless barrage has left many questioning the future, even forcing some to reconsider the idea of bringing children into a world that feels increasingly unpredictable and hostile.

The cumulative impact of global turmoil has left many with a growing sense of despair about where society is headed. Feelings of disconnection and overwhelm surround the relentless cycle of violence, political divides, and social instability. It's important to remember this is a natural, human reaction to chaos and uncertainty. Events characterized by division and conflict often lead to a sense of helplessness, as if individual actions are too small to make a difference. Yet, it is precisely in these moments of despair that the need for empathy and connection becomes most urgent.

Let's get one thing straight: I am incredibly progressive. From the very beginning, I acknowledge my personal bias while simultaneously declaring that empathy is the foundation for societal change. This is a hill I am willing to die on. There is no alternative to collective care—there isn't a world in which I'd consciously choose to exclude people who are systemically marginalized. I hope in reading this, you'll feel that way, too.

Throughout this book, you will read a collection of stories mixed with psychology and sociopolitics. It's a balance of storytelling and history, the very framework that has carried our collective memory for centuries. Through these stories, I aim to highlight the growing empathy deficit *and* suggest ways to solve it.

Each "character" in this book is real. Their stories, their beliefs, their messages—all moments in their personal histories that I was fortunate enough to bear witness to. Their names have been changed to protect their privacy. In telling their stories, I often jump timelines. Do not try to connect the dots. The stories are told in an order that I think will benefit you the most, not chronologically. You do not need to experience my order of events to gain from it.

And, finally, I want to acknowledge that no system is perfect. The examples of community that I share throughout this book are not end-all-be-all solutions. They are frameworks from which we can draw. Small parts of a larger collective that can better serve humankind. We don't have to recreate systems in their entirety. In fact, doing so would be inconsequential; we've learned these systems eventually break down. Why, then, would we try to recreate them? Instead, we should learn from them.

My goal for you is simple but mighty: I want you to learn to sink into the present moment, experience it fully, and feel it deeply. I want you to cherish the small moments and find comfort in stillness. I want you to extend kindness and care without expectation. I want you to connect—wholly, meaningfully, and without reservation—with yourself and with others. Basically, I want you to be a good human, and I want humans to be good to you in return.

It may be my personal belief that we are capable of so much more, but people have proven time and time again that we are stronger when we're together. Without each other, we lack the very thing that makes life worth living: connection. Once you realize that, you'll never look at life the same.

I'll see you on the other side.

1

The Kindness We Forgot

How often do we stop to help someone without expecting anything in return? We're taught from a young age that small, selfless acts of kindness create meaningful change.

"Treat others the way you want to be treated."

"Sharing is caring."

"Be kind; you never know what someone else is going through."

"A little kindness goes a long way."

We're conditioned from a young age to be kind and help others, yet somewhere along the way, many of us stop practicing what we were taught. Why is that?

As children, we accept these lessons without hesitation—sharing a snack with a friend, comforting a classmate who feels left out, or offering a hand to someone who falls on the playground. These moments are instinctual, driven by a pure understanding that kindness is both natural and necessary. But as we grow older, our relationship with care begins to shift. We don't unlearn kindness outright, but we start to question when, how, and to whom we should offer it.

Part of this shift comes from the transition into adult realism—a growing awareness that the world isn't always kind in return. We learn that generosity can be exploited, not everyone will reciprocate our goodwill, and self-preservation often takes priority. The innocence of childhood, when care is freely given, fades into a more guarded approach: Be kind, but careful.

At the same time, we are shaped by a Western culture that glorifies independence. Success becomes synonymous with self-sufficiency and personal achievement. Childhood teaches us to lean on each other—to share, ask for help, and offer it in return—but, somewhere along the way, that interdependence is replaced with isolation. We're told to focus on ourselves and be strong, and, slowly, care becomes something we offer only when it's convenient, if at all. But in a time of rising loneliness, burnout, and division, this departure from care isn't just a personal loss; it's a collective threat.

Even with all these cultural shifts, our capacity for unconditional care hasn't disappeared. It's still there, offering kindness without expecting anything in return. And in a world so often fueled by self-interest, that kind of care is radical. It creates authentic, meaningful connection. It reminds us of what's possible. But if we're being honest, it's scarce. We've been taught to chase self-reliance and personal success, even when they cost us community. Care is now a transaction—support that we offer when there's something to receive in return. Help a friend, donate to a cause, lend a hand at work . . . all while quietly wondering, *What do I get out of this?*

But what happens when care is only given with expectation? When kindness becomes a currency to be traded rather than a gift freely offered? To put it bluntly: We begin to withhold it. We ration our compassion, subconsciously calculating whether someone is "deserving" before extending a hand. We hesitate in moments where we once would have acted instinctively, and slowly, the world hardens. We scroll past stories of suffering, convincing ourselves there's nothing we can do. We see someone begging on the street and assume they failed, rarely considering the systemic forces that push people into the streets—forces that the majority of us have experienced to some degree, like unaffordable housing, medical debt, job insecurity, and barriers to mental health care. The spaces between us widen despite our similarities, and apathy replaces the instinct to care, making us less likely to reach out, help, and see ourselves in one another.

I'll be honest, there are moments when I struggle to extend care, too. A few blocks from my apartment, an old armory was recently converted into a homeless shelter. Many of the residents are living with active addiction. Because drug use isn't permitted inside, people often use just outside the shelter's doors—on the sidewalks I walk each morning with my dog. I've found myself tightening, judging, pulling away. Even entertaining thoughts like, *In this neighborhood? This shouldn't be happening here.* I've convinced myself it's about safety, but the truth is, it's discomfort. My nervous system flares, so my compassion flattens. And in those moments, I forget that the people I pass aren't just stories of addiction—they're humans trying to survive. People trying to cope with *real world* issues that I'm privileged not to face. Even as a therapist, I have to continuously practice care, and it doesn't always come easy.

And that's how it happens. Before we know it, we become strangers—even to the people standing right beside us. But if isolation and self-preservation were truly our natural state, humanity wouldn't have survived this long. In reality, we are wired for connection. Across disciplines—evolutionary biology, neuroscience, and psychology—research consistently shows that altruism is deeply embedded in human nature.

Evolutionary biologists argue that cooperation, not competition, is what allowed our species to thrive. Kin selection theory (Hamilton, 1964) suggests that humans evolved to protect and support those genetically related to them, ensuring the survival of shared genes. But reciprocal altruism (Trivers, 1971) explains why humans extend care beyond family bonds—our ancestors who helped others were more likely to receive help in return, increasing their chances of survival. This instinct for mutual aid laid the foundation for the tribal bonds that still shape human behavior today.

This deep-rooted instinct for mutual aid is a topic I often discuss in therapy. Clients tend to struggle with their innate need for connection and the modern world's emphasis on independence and self-sufficiency. They report feelings of loneliness, difficulty asking for help even when struggling, and guilt for relying on others—symptoms of a society that glorifies self-reliance while neglecting our fundamental need for connection. I remind them that their longing for community isn't a weakness; it's written into their biology. Evolutionary psychology helps us understand that we are not wired to navigate life alone; we are social creatures, shaped by thousands of years of cooperation and interdependence.

Early hunter-gatherer societies thrived not because of individual success, but because of shared responsibilities and communal care. Survival depended on collaboration—one person might have been an expert at tracking prey, while another knew how to identify edible plants, and another had the skill to craft tools. These groups understood something that we have largely forgotten today: Caring for others wasn't just an act of kindness; it was essential for survival.

In sessions with clients, I often reference this communal history to challenge the modern belief that asking for help, or offering it freely, is somehow a sign of weakness. I've worked with people who feel ashamed for needing support, as if self-reliance is the only acceptable path. But when we reframe their struggles through the lens of evolutionary psychology, clients begin to see that their desire for connection isn't a flaw; it's a fundamental human trait. Just as our ancestors depended on one another for food, shelter, and safety, we, too, need relationships, care, and trust to thrive.

Yet, in today's world, this evolutionary truth is often ignored. Instead of recognizing interdependence, we are taught to prioritize individual success over collective well-being. The ancient bonds of cooperation are overshadowed by hyper-independence, making acts of unconditional care feel unnatural or even unnecessary. But the reality is, when we suppress our need for connection, we go against the wiring that helped our species survive.

From an early age, we are predisposed to help others. Studies on infants show that even before they can speak, babies demonstrate a preference for helpful behavior (Hamlin et al., 2007). This suggests that altruism is not something we learn—it's something we are born with. But if caring for others is so deeply ingrained, why do we so often resist it? The answer isn't that we've lost our ability to care—it's that modern life has conditioned us to override it.

Acts of care, once seen as essential to survival, are now framed as distractions, weaknesses, or inefficiencies in a society that prioritizes achievement, self-sufficiency, and success over communal well-being. We are subtly trained to suppress emotional responses that don't serve individual advancement—pausing to help a stranger is seen as an inconvenience, while asking for help ourselves can feel like a failure. Over time, this conditioning dulls our sensitivity to the needs of others, making detachment easier and empathy harder to access.

The good news? Just because empathy feels harder to reach doesn't mean it's disappeared. Our brains are still wired for connection, even if we've been taught to suppress it. The pull toward care and compassion still exists beneath the surface, embedded in the very architecture of our minds.

At a neurological level, mirror neurons—discovered by Rizzolatti et al. (1996)—fire both when we perform an action and when we see someone else experiencing it. This mirroring effect allows us to feel another person's pain as if it were our own, creating the basis for empathy. Additionally, acts of kindness activate the brain's reward system, releasing dopamine and oxytocin, sometimes referred to as the "helper's high" (Luks & Payne, 1992). This biological reinforcement encourages prosocial behavior, strengthening social bonds and increasing overall well-being.

Though I'd like to believe that kindness is universal, in reality, our care is not evenly distributed. Empathy is selective, shaped by unconscious biases, social conditioning, and group dynamics. We might instinctively feel compassion for a struggling friend, yet hesitate to help a stranger. We donate to causes that feel personally meaningful while scrolling past others without a second thought. This isn't because we lack compassion—it's because, whether we realize it or not, we categorize people into groups, and those categorizations influence how much empathy we offer.

I witnessed this biased sub-categorization firsthand while standing in immigration lines in Italy. The room was filled with people from all over the world, each of us grouped together under the same label: immigrants. And yet, we were not treated the same. As a white woman of Italian descent, I blended in. Immigration officers spoke to me first, processing my paperwork without suspicion. But others—those whose accents, skin tones, or countries of origin marked them as "outsiders"—were met with scrutiny and impatience, if not ignored altogether. The difference was unmistakable. Despite the fact that we were all there for the same reason, belonging to certain groups seemed to make some people more worthy of kindness than others.

This pattern of selective empathy isn't limited to individual interactions; it plays out on a global scale, shaping policies, humanitarian efforts, and even public opinion. One of the most striking examples in recent years is the global refugee crisis.

According to social identity theory (Turner et al., 1979), people categorize themselves and others into groups, prioritizing those they perceive as part of their 'in-group' while showing less concern for 'out-groups.' The theory suggests that humans derive a sense of self from the groups they belong to, whether those are based on culture, nationality, race, religion, political affiliation, or shared experiences. These groups provide a sense of belonging and identity, but they also create division between "us" and "them."

Research has shown that the way refugees are portrayed in the media directly impacts public empathy. When refugees are framed as desperate families fleeing war and violence, support for aid increases, but when they are framed as "illegal aliens" or "threats to national security," as is popular amongst right-wing rhetoric, the response shifts to fear, resistance, and exclusion (Esses et al., 2013). These narratives shape public perception, influencing which groups are deemed worthy of help and which are met with hostility.

It's easy to believe that we judge people solely as individuals, but in reality, our perception of others is deeply influenced by who we believe they are, where they come from, and whether they "belong" in our current world. These judgements—sometimes conscious, sometimes subconscious—determine who we are willing to extend care to and who we keep at a distance. When Ukrainian refugees fled war in 2022, many Western nations opened their borders and provided extensive aid, while refugees from Syria, Afghanistan, and parts of Africa have historically faced stricter immigration policies and greater public resistance. The difference? One group is more likely to be perceived as part of the in-group due to cultural, racial, or political similarities, while the other is viewed as just that—*other*.

The refugee crisis underscores the urgency of moving beyond selective empathy. If we are only willing to extend care to those who feel familiar or "like us," we reinforce division. My observations of the Italian immigration process stuck with me. It was much deeper than bureaucracy—this was about belonging. The immigration officers weren't just processing documents; they were making split-second decisions about who deserved their warmth and who didn't. But these decisions weren't random. They were shaped by an unconscious tendency we all share: the instinct to sort people into groups, deciding who is one of us and who is not.

The way we categorize others doesn't just influence who we empathize with; it also determines who we feel obligated to help. Reciprocity norms, one of the fundamental principles of human interaction, suggest that people are more likely to help those from whom they expect something in return. This expectation isn't always conscious, but it's deeply ingrained in how we navigate relationships. In essence, we are conditioned to extend care where we believe it will eventually be repaid.

This helps explain why in-group favoritism is so strong—we tend to support those who are most likely to return the favor, reinforcing the bonds within our own social circles. But when it comes to people in the out-group, those we perceive as different from us, the expectation of reciprocity weakens, making care feel optional rather than instinctual. This selective generosity mirrors what I witnessed in the immigration line: Some people were met with warmth and understanding, while others were dismissed, as if their presence didn't warrant the same level of care.

True connection—genuine human empathy—cannot exist only within the walls of reciprocity. If we only help when we expect something in return, we reduce kindness to a transaction rather than a reflection of our shared humanity. Social identity theory explains why we instinctively categorize people, and reciprocity norms explain why we selectively help, but both of these forces can, and *should*, be challenged.

In a world driven by self-interest, unconditional care offers another way—one that crosses social divides and reminds us that connection isn't earned—it's given. Extending care without conditions pushes back against a transactional culture and returns us to a simple truth: Our survival depends on our ability to see and support each other. True care means recognizing our shared humanity, not just when it's easy, but especially when it's hard.

If we rethink how we engage with care—if we extend kindness without expectation, even beyond the boundaries of our in-groups—what happens next? Acts of kindness have a way of echoing outward, shaping not only the lives of those who receive them, but also those who witness them. There's a reason why social scientists have studied the effects of generosity for decades, and why countless books and films center around the power of human connection. These moments, however small, reveal something fundamental about human behavior: Kindness isn't just a virtue; it's an active force that shapes how we engage with the world.

A moment of unexpected generosity can shift someone's perspective, reinforce trust in others, or inspire them to pass that kindness forward. At an individual level, selfless acts boost well-being, strengthen relationships, and reinforce our sense of purpose. At a community level, they create stronger social bonds and encourage cultures of mutual support. And on a larger scale, they lay the foundation for a more compassionate society—one where empathy isn't seen as weakness, but as a guiding principle.

Most of us have experienced the impact of a stranger's kindness, but we rarely recognize in the moment just how deeply it will shape us. I think about a man named Jack often, a man whose selfless act of care altered my understanding of what it means to show up for others.

It happened in an airport. I was young, alone, and stranded in a foreign country after missing my connecting flight to Milan. Panic settled in as I fumbled with my phone, trying to explain the situation to my mother—I had just landed in Lisbon, but I missed my flight to Milan. It was my first time flying alone, and I wasn't just visiting; I was moving to another country. The weight of that reality hit me all at once. Everything about this journey felt uncertain, and now, before I had even arrived, I was already lost. That's when Jack turned around.

He was a man with curly blond hair and thick-rimmed glasses, who looked like the love child of Napoleon Dynamite and Austin Powers. A niche reference, but shockingly accurate. Without hesitation, Jack grabbed my phone and said, "Let me help you." Who was I to argue? I was stranded, sleep-deprived, and one minor inconvenience away from a full-blown airport meltdown—though if you asked Jack, he'd probably say I was already deep into the meltdown.

I'd later discover that Jack was a program analyst for the United Nations—someone used to solving high-stakes, global issues. But at that moment, his mission was to get one panicked twenty-something from Lisbon to Milan. In fluent Portuguese, Jack rebooked my flight, and for the next seven hours, we sat together in an airport Burger King, trading life stories and drifting in and out of the kind of half-sleep that one only gets from full-body exhaustion. Jack had nothing to gain from helping me. He wasn't trying to prove anything, and he didn't expect anything in return. He helped simply because he could—and to this day, I still don't know how many languages he speaks.

That single act, offering his time, his expertise, and his presence, eased my immediate distress. More than that, it reinforced something deeper: When people extend care freely, it has the power to create a lasting imprint, shifting our perspective on how we engage with the world. Jack's kindness fundamentally shifted my understanding of social responsibility. We actually *do* owe one other kindness, and that's just the bare minimum.

This is the altruism effect in action. Research shows that engaging in selfless acts benefits both the recipient and the giver. Altruistic behavior activates the brain's reward system, reducing stress and increasing happiness (Post, 2005). It also strengthens social bonds, reinforcing a sense of connection and trust, even among strangers. When we experience care without expectation, we are more likely to pay it forward, creating a ripple effect that extends far beyond a single act of kindness.

By now, you might be wondering if kindness is so deeply embedded in human nature, why do so many of us struggle to practice it consistently? The answer is quite simple: scarcity, fatigue, and fear. There simply isn't enough space in our modern lives to extend care to others, and the current state of the world creates compassion fatigue—a psychological response that occurs when people are exposed to too much suffering. Much of society is experiencing emotional burnout, and what do we do when we're burned out? We retreat into individualism as a form of self-preservation. It's a vicious cycle of disconnection—one that reinforces apathy, isolates us from one another, and makes acts of care feel like burdens rather than instincts. The more we withdraw, the harder it becomes to extend kindness, and the more kindness fades from our daily lives.

Yet, despite these barriers, care is still possible. If we recognize the forces that hold us back, we can begin to challenge them. We can carve out time, even in small moments. We can safeguard against compassion fatigue by focusing on what we *can* do rather than what we can't. We can offer kindness anyway, even when we're unsure if it will be returned.

I'm optimistic that care isn't disappearing—it's just quieter than the chaos that surrounds it. We're too distracted to see it, but small, selfless acts happen around us every day. In a world that prioritizes what's urgent, dramatic, or divisive, kindness often fades into the background. But when we start paying attention, we begin to see it everywhere: the stranger who holds the door open, the person who lets someone merge into traffic, the colleague who checks in when they sense something is off.

The more we notice these moments, the easier it becomes to practice care ourselves. When we attune to kindness, we train our brains to look for it—*and* to create it. Just as negativity bias conditions us to focus on threat, we can condition ourselves to recognize generosity, warmth, and connection. Care is contagious, and by simply paying attention to it, we strengthen our own capacity to extend it.

We hold on tightly to control, certainty, and the idea that we must always be productive, but connection, care, and even joy often require the opposite: a willingness to let go. In the next chapter, we explore what it means to release the need for control, embrace the present moment, and create space for the kind of care that is freely given—not as an obligation, but as an instinct.

2

The More You Let Go, The More You Feel

M ost of us are always elsewhere. We scroll while we eat, check emails during conversations, and plan tomorrow while today slips through our fingers. But in chasing efficiency and distraction, we lose something essential: our ability to actually *feel* our lives as we live them.

Yet there are places in the world where distraction simply isn't an option—where the present moment demands your attention. Antarctica is one of those places, and I was fortunate enough to experience it firsthand.

I expected Antarctica to be breathtaking, but nothing prepared me for the overwhelming stillness of it all. The vast, ice-covered landscape stretched endlessly in every direction, untouched and indifferent to the noise of the world I had left behind. No notifications. No obligations. Just the sound of the wind cutting through glaciers and the occasional crack of ice shifting in the distance. It was here that I met Maren.

Maren was an expedition leader, but more importantly, she was the kind of person whose presence instantly puts you at ease. The two weren't inherently connected, but to her advantage, they complemented each other perfectly. Her steady presence and calm demeanor served as a quiet reminder to not let our emotions—or our habits of distraction—pull us away from the experience itself.

Thanks to Maren, I didn't just see Antarctica. I felt it. I remember the crunch of ice beneath my boots, the soft splashes of penguins diving into the water, and the sheer vastness of it all that made everything feel sacred. Maren taught us that presence wasn't just about looking, but absorbing and fully being *there* without letting our minds pull us elsewhere.

She spoke often about the art of presence, which she described as the power of experiencing a moment as it is rather than as we expect it to be. Watching her move through the icy landscape, it was clear that Maren was accomplishing far more than the expeditions that were assigned to her—she was teaching people how to slow down, to notice, and to simply *be*, something even I struggle to demonstrate as a therapist.

I was one of the first of two hundred passengers to step foot onto the continent during that trip. The crew had set up a row of foldable camp chairs near the shoreline, a quiet invitation to pause. Maren immediately gestured toward them.

"Sit," she encouraged, "Just watch."

I hesitated. The urge to reach for my phone—to document proof that I was here—felt almost instinctual, in a sick, content-driven type of way. But something in her tone gave me pause, so I sat. I let the cold air settle into my bones, and I soaked it all in exactly as it was. No filter, no frame, and a surprisingly dulled impulse to preserve it beyond memory.

Within minutes, a group of gentoo penguins approached, playful and uninhibited, their movements so absurdly endearing that I actually laughed out loud. By sheer chance, I caught Maren's smile out of the corner of my eye.

"When you let go of the need to hold on," she said, "you actually experience more."

When we're constantly pulled away from the present, mindfulness offers a way back—to ourselves, to each other, and to the experiences that make life meaningful.

The Science of Mindfulness: Why Presence Matters

Mindfulness, at its core, is the practice of intentionally drawing awareness to the present moment without judgment. While it may sound simple, its impact on the brain and body is profound. Neuroscience shows that a consistent mindfulness practice strengthens neural connections in the prefrontal cortex, the part of the brain responsible for decision-making, emotional regulation, and focus (Tang, Hölzel & Posner, 2015). At the same time, it reduces activity in the amygdala, the region associated with fear and stress responses, leading to lower levels of anxiety and greater emotional resilience over time.

When we're present, our brain stops anticipating the next task or replaying past mistakes. Instead, it settles into what researchers call the "being mode," allowing us to respond rather than react, and observe rather than judge. This shift calms the nervous system and increases cognitive flexibility, which is the brain's ability to adapt to change, regulate emotions, and think creatively.

Studies have also found that mindfulness enhances interpersonal functioning. People who practice mindfulness are more attuned to emotional cues, more likely to express empathy, and better able to manage conflict (Carson et al., 2004). In other words, presence doesn't just change how we feel—it changes how we relate.

Mindfulness-based interventions are pillars in mental health treatment and for good reason. They reduce symptoms of depression, improve sleep, and increase overall well-being (Kabat-Zinn, 2003). Beyond clinical outcomes, mindfulness returns something that we desperately need: the ability to actually *feel* what we're experiencing in real-time. Fully, viscerally, and without distraction. The vibration in your chest when a crowd sings in unison at a concert. The warmth of the sun on your face after days of gray skies. That belly-deep laugh you share with a friend that leaves your cheeks feeling sore. Learning to notice and experience these sensations to their fullest extent is mindfulness.

Presence isn't passive—it's an active form of participation. It invites us to notice the details we usually miss, like the rhythm of a conversation or the slight shift in someone's tone. These are the subtle yet powerful cues that ground us in the here and now. The details we lose when our attention is scattered or hijacked by distraction.

The Cost of Disconnection

Despite having more ways to connect than ever before, many of us feel increasingly detached—from ourselves, from others, and from the world around us. We exist on autopilot. We scroll through curated highlight reels of other people's lives while feeling disengaged from our own. We answer emails during dinner, half-listen during conversations, and doom scroll during our rare, free moments, unsure of how to just *be*.

This level of disconnection runs deeper than our emotions. It's physiological. When we live in a state of constant distraction, our nervous systems remain activated. We stay on high alert, toggling between tasks and thoughts without ever landing in a "neutral calm." The result? Chronic stress, reduced attention spans, and a growing sense of dissatisfaction. In fact, one of the most cited studies on happiness found that people are significantly less happy when their minds are wandering than when they are focused on what they're doing—even if the activity itself is mundane (Killingsworth & Gilbert, 2010).

Presence, on the other hand, anchors us. It allows us to feel more alive because we're actually *in* our lives. It gives us access to joy, gratitude, and connection, the very emotions that become difficult to reach when we're mentally elsewhere. And when we're disconnected from ourselves, we inevitably disconnect from others. We miss emotional cues. We fail to notice when someone's energy shifts. We don't hear what's being said between the lines.

Over time, these distractions erode the foundations of our relationships. Partners become strangers. Friends grow distant. Community begins to feel like a performance rather than a source of support. As our digital worlds expand, our real-world connections often shrink. And when we lose presence, we lose the very thing that makes connection possible: attention.

Still, our impulse to reconnect with presence is more natural than we give ourselves credit for. I've started to notice small, intuitive ways people attempt to reclaim mindfulness in their daily lives—young adults placing their phones in the middle of the dinner table and agreeing that whoever reaches for their phone first pays the bill, or "silent book clubs," where people gather just to read in each other's company—these trends are quiet acts of resistance against a world that constantly pulls us away from the moment.

Stand-up comic Des Bishop captured this beautifully during a set at the Comedy Cellar in New York. "When I was a teenager, nobody mentioned the word mindfulness," he said. "And do you know why that was? Because we were mindful half of every day—we didn't have a choice. We didn't have a cable service in our pocket. You waited for somebody, and you *waited*. Mindfulness. You were on the bus, and you were on the bus watching condensation drip. Mindfulness." What was once inherent is now something we have to fight for.

In my work with couples, I see this theme embed itself in relationships, driving couples apart. One of the most common beliefs I help couples unlearn is the assumption that "time together" equates to quality time. Spoiler: It doesn't. Sitting on the couch while scrolling your phones doesn't count. Neither does binging a show while you're each in your own digital world. Presence means intentionally creating space for one another—looking up, checking in, being fully there. No distractions. No divided attention. Just presence.

The Role of Presence in Connection

In relationships, presence serves as the foundation of meaningful connection. To be truly present with someone is to signal, without words, "I'm here. I'm listening. You matter." In a world where so many of us feel unseen, this kind of attention becomes one of the most powerful gifts we can offer.

Presence doesn't just deepen relationships—it creates them. It feeds intimacy, trust, and emotional safety. Whether it's the way a partner turns toward you during a vulnerable conversation or a friend who listens without distraction, presence communicates care in a way that words alone cannot, and often, it's the absence of presence that causes the most pain. Think of a child whose parent is physically there, but emotionally unreachable, or a romantic partner who's always on their phone during dinner. We feel the loss of connection even when someone is right beside us because attention is the currency of connection, and without it, relationships go hungry.

Presence allows us to tune into the subtleties—the pause before someone shares something vulnerable, the shift in tone that reveals unspoken emotion, the moments of silence that don't feel empty, but full. These small signals get lost when we're distracted. We might hear the words someone says, but miss what they actually mean. We might respond, but not attune.

I often remind clients that connection doesn't require grand gestures. It starts with eye contact. By putting the phone away. Choosing to be here, fully, even when "here" feels quiet or slow or emotionally charged, and especially when it would be easier to "check out." Connection lives in those small, present moments, and when we show up for them, we remind each other what it feels like to be truly seen.

Learning to Let Go: The Paradox of Presence

Presence requires surrender, and in a society that rewards productivity, certainty, and control, surrender doesn't come easily. Most of us are taught, whether explicitly or not, that if we don't capture the moment, it didn't happen. Sayings like "phone eats first" and "pics or it didn't happen" reinforce this idea. We snap photos to prove we were there, post about our joy to validate it, and try to preserve fleeting moments as if our memory alone won't be enough, but the paradox of presence is that the less we try to hold onto a moment, the more deeply we experience it.

Trying to preserve a moment often removes us from it entirely. We become spectators of our own lives, chasing the illusion of permanence in a world that is, by nature, ever-changing. We hold on so tightly, trying to freeze time or control outcomes, that we forget to live when we're actually in it.

Letting go doesn't mean letting life pass us by. It means releasing the impulse to curate, to control, and to perfect. To be fully present is to trust that the moment—in its raw and unscripted form—is enough, without needing to capture or control it. When we do this, we loosen our grip and open ourselves to something more expansive. A depth of experience that can't be replicated through a screen or summarized in a caption. A quiet, grounding kind of joy that lives in the being, not the documenting. In Antarctica, Maren taught me that presence isn't passive; it's intentional. And the present moment asks us to let go—not to lose something, but to experience it more completely.

Of course, presence requires more of us than simply putting our phones away. It asks for something deeper: to sit with what's *actually* here, even if it's uncomfortable. That's what we're often avoiding when we reach for distraction. We fear what we'll feel if we stop reaching, stop editing, stop performing. Embarrassment? Uncertainty? Boredom? All feelings we desperately try to ignore.

But presence isn't a reward for a perfect life. It's the practice of being with life exactly as it is, even when it's messy or quiet or unresolved. That's what makes it so radical. So healing.

The Final Goodbye

When our ship returned to port in Ushuaia, everything felt quieter. The air was still, the sky a solid blue with very few clouds to disrupt it, and the usual chatter on board was replaced with something new—an unspoken awareness that we were leaving something behind that we couldn't quite name. That morning, one of the expedition leaders led the group in a moment of reflection. We took turns passing the microphone around the room, sharing the experiences and the lessons we were taking with us. It was an opportunity for emotional closure after ten days of heightened adventure.

One of the guests shared how meaningful her new relationships were. She admitted to struggling with making friends as an adult. Earlier on the trip, that same girl pulled me aside and shared something more personal—she lost one of her closest friends when she was a teenager.

Another guest, one whose presence naturally brightened the room, shared her guiding message that later became a theme in my own life: *Feel the fear, but do it anyway.* She embarked on this journey to Antarctica as a way to push herself beyond her comfort zone in the weeks leading up to her divorce.

Someone else shared that our trip to Antarctica was the first time she had felt true joy and lightness since her father's diagnosis. After months of caring for him, he encouraged her to go, despite her fear of her father passing while she was away. What began as a single journey to the end of the earth turned into something much bigger. She stayed onboard for two additional voyages—one returning to Antarctica, and another northbound to the Falkland Islands.

With each reflection, it was clear that the trip offered far more than an escape from daily life. It opened something in all of us. We came for the adventure, the landscapes, the stories we'd tell when we returned home, but we left with something quieter and more permanent: a sense of renewal and a reminder that connection, both to others and to ourselves, is still possible in a world that so often pulls us apart. For me, that shift began long before we returned to port. It started with Maren.

I hadn't prepared for how hard it would be to say good-bye—not to the landscape, but to her. Maren led our expedition, yes . . . but, more importantly, she anchored us to the present moment, reminding us how to pay attention to our experiences before the moments pass. As we boarded the buses to the airport, I walked over to Maren. There was no dramatic send-off, no grand farewell—just the kind of quiet recognition that follows a meaningful connection.

"I just want you to know," I said, already blinking back tears, "this trip wouldn't have been what it was without you." She pulled me into a hug, and, for a moment, neither of us spoke. There was nothing else to say. The emotion between us didn't need translating.

We hadn't shared a life-changing conversation or a deeply personal exchange. What made Maren's presence unforgettable was its consistency—her ability to make people feel calm, steady, and anchored in a world that constantly pulls us away from ourselves. She didn't just lead us through Antarctica. She led us back into the present moment, again and again.

That's the thing about presence. It's easy to overlook when you're in it, but once you've experienced it, you feel its absence everywhere. Maren's words often come back to me:

"When you let go of the need to hold on, you actually experience more."

She was right. The more I tried to cling to the feeling of Antarctica—to imprint it, record it, preserve it—the more it slipped away. But the moments when I surrendered, when I stopped grasping and simply paid attention, those are the ones I remember most. Presence doesn't last forever, but it definitely leaves a trace.

Presence isn't something we stumble into. It's a body-mind connection that we consciously have to choose. One way to practice this is through what I now call a "drop-in." It's a small, intentional pause to fully notice a moment without documenting, analyzing, or narrating it. It's noticing the sensation of a breeze as it blows by. It's listening to the cycling of your dog's inhales and exhales when they're asleep next to you. The warmth of a mug after you've just poured your coffee. No phone to record it. No agenda. Just a brief arrival to your senses.

Let that moment be enough. Let it imprint itself on you. Eventually, you'll find it becomes part of a ritual.

3

The Dance Between Fear and Freedom

In 2017, I was standing at the edge of the dance-floor in Milan's La Balera dell'Ortica, an old-school dance-hall-turned-modern-bar housed in a former railway station. Rooted in Italian history, La Balera welcomed railway employees seeking an escape from post-war hardship and Benito Mussolini's rise to power. Back then, people gathered to dance liscio, an Italian equivalent of ballroom dancing. But that day, when I stood on the edge of the dancefloor at that same dance hall, I watched my friend Matteo glide across the room in a state of euphoria with a more upbeat and playful swing.

Matteo, one of the many talented and accomplished dancers on the dancefloor, extended his hand and asked me to dance. Every fiber of my body wanted to say no—not because I didn't want to dance, but because I didn't want to be *seen*. I was hyper-aware of everything from my posture to the way my arms felt beside my body. A familiar voice inside me, one that was sharp, skeptical, and protective, whispered, *Don't draw attention to yourself.*

I've spent most of my life negotiating with my inner critic. It shows up in moments like this, trying to keep me safe by making me small. And for a long time, it worked. I stayed on the sidelines. I avoided being perceived. I told myself it was easier that way, but in that moment—with music pouring through the speakers and Matteo's hand still outstretched—something clicked. The very instinct designed to protect me had become the thing that isolated me most.

Maybe it's because I finally had nothing left to lose. I had just left an abusive relationship that chipped away at my sense of self until I no longer trusted my own instincts. I'd spent the past year walking on eggshells, trying to make myself small, quiet, and agreeable enough to survive. When I finally escaped that relationship, I didn't feel free—I was empty. Like the version of me that once existed had been carefully deconstructed, piece by piece, with nothing tangible to replace what was missing. So when Matteo reached out his hand, maybe some part of me recognized that I was already in the process of rebuilding, and that moment, however small, was a step toward reclaiming something I had lost: the right to take up space.

I took Matteo's hand, and in doing so, I stepped into a version of myself I hadn't met yet. She didn't need to be perfect or composed, and she didn't stress about being "cool" or belonging. That girl was present. Open.

We often think of openness as a personality trait, but it's a choice. A stance we take toward the world around us. To stay open, especially when we've been hurt or disappointed, requires courage. It means allowing space for uncertainty, risking vulnerability, and choosing curiosity, even when it's easier to shut down.

Facing the Inner Critic

We all carry a voice inside us that tries to protect us. Sometimes it's quiet and cautious. Other times, it's loud, harsh, and unforgiving. For me, my inner critic often sounded like, *Don't embarrass yourself. Don't make a scene. Don't give people a reason to judge you.* I used to think this voice was rooted in shyness or insecurity, but over time, I realized it wasn't just about fear—it was connected to my identity.

When we grow up in a world that teaches us how to measure our worth by how well we fit in, we learn to contort ourselves. We smooth out the edges that make us unique. We observe what's "acceptable" within our families, our communities, and our cultures, and we adapt accordingly. Social identity theory helps explain this phenomenon—how we define ourselves by the groups we belong to, and how we learn which behaviors strengthen our membership in those groups. Over time, we internalize those rules. We learn what earns praise and what invites rejection. We create an inner critic that enforces those boundaries for us, long after the original threat has passed.

For many of us, especially women, the critic doesn't just whisper—it polices. It tells us to stay small, quiet, and agreeable. To be liked instead of real. We're told to avoid taking up too much space physically and emotionally. And when we do take risks, when we raise our voices, express strong opinions, or, in my case, accept an invitation to dance—our inner critic chimes in, warning us not to stand out.

Matteo danced like someone who was never told to shrink himself, though I know that's likely untrue. His movements were fluid, confident, and magnetic, not in a look-at-me kind of way, but in the way that makes you want to join in. He didn't perform for approval. He danced because it felt *good*. Dancing connected Matteo to something joyful and real. Watching him, I realized how rarely I gave myself permission to move freely, to take up space without apology. Matteo's openness wasn't just an invitation to dance; it was an invitation to challenge the version of myself I had grown so used to editing.

The irony is, in trying to belong, we often lose the very parts of ourselves that make connection possible. We try to preempt rejection by shrinking ourselves into someone more palatable. We don't realize, though, that trying not to be seen often costs us the ability to truly see ourselves.

When I stepped onto that dance floor in Milan, I let go of a version of myself I had outgrown. For a moment, I ignored my compulsion to protect and to hide. That choice didn't silence my inner critic, but it did do something more important: It reminded me that I don't have to actually *listen* to the voice. Openness requires us to notice the voice and act anyway, not because we're fearless, but because we're ready to live from a different place—one rooted not in fear of being seen, but in the desire to be fully known.

The Psychology of Openness

We crave maps to better understand ourselves. Personality tests, horoscopes, attachment styles—they help us make sense of who we are and how we move through the world. But the danger comes when we mistake the map for the territory.

One of the most widely accepted maps in psychology is the Big Five personality framework (Costa & McCrae, 1992), which includes traits like conscientiousness, extraversion, agreeableness, and neuroticism. Openness to experience is one of them. It refers to a person's creativity, imagination, curiosity, and comfort with new ideas or experiences.

It's a useful framework, but like any model, it has limitations. Most of the research behind it comes from WEIRD populations—Western, Educated, Industrialized, Rich, and Democratic—so it doesn't capture the full range of human complexity. It's just one lens, not the whole picture. Still, it helps us understand how openness shows up in our daily lives, and why it may come more naturally to some than others.

Frameworks, Identity, and Flexibility

As a therapist, I've found that personality frameworks, while helpful, can also become harmful if we treat them as fixed truths rather than tools for exploration. I don't administer personality tests, but when clients ask to explore frameworks like Myers-Briggs or Human Design, I welcome the conversation because they often reveal something valuable: a desire for self-understanding. We naturally seek out language to explain who we are and how we relate to the world—if we want to get really meta, that's why most social constructs and organized religions exist, but we'll save that conversation for the next chapter. Regardless of framework, I offer the same reminder to *take what resonates, and let go of what doesn't.* These frameworks are maps, not mandates. They can offer insight, but they shouldn't box us in.

When we allow ourselves to remain open—to new frameworks, to discomfort, or to unlearning—we start to see that connection isn't built through rigid identities, but through shared moments that remind us we're not alone. Openness, in particular, is a trait that often surprises people. I've worked with clients who once described themselves as "rigid," "anxious," or "closed off," only to later discover a deep reservoir of curiosity and courage within them. It wasn't that they lacked openness—they just hadn't been in environments where openness felt safe, supported, or even possible.

I think that's true for many of us. We don't struggle with openness because we're incapable of it, but because we've been taught, consciously or not, that it comes with risk. New experiences might expose us. Vulnerability might make us feel foolish. And so, we retreat to the familiar, telling ourselves stories about who we are and what we can't do, all for the purpose of "belonging."

Here's the truth: We're not meant to be static. When we allow ourselves to try something new—to travel alone, to dance, to start over—we open ourselves to more than just the experience itself. We open the door to who we might become.

Overcoming Disconnection Through Shared Experiences

While much of modern life, at least in the West, is designed around efficiency and individualism, human beings are wired for something else entirely: connection. And not just connection in the form of conversation or companionship, but connection through doing. Movement, rhythm, ritual, and storytelling. Across cultures and centuries, we've gathered to dance, cook, sing, and share. These shared experiences weren't seen as luxuries or hobbies. They were culture itself.

Evolutionary psychology helps explain this. Our ancestors depended on group cohesion to survive. From tribal rituals to seasonal celebrations, shared experiences fostered trust and reinforced belonging. These communal activities helped groups align values, coordinate efforts, and maintain harmony. In fact, anthropologists argue that cultural expressions like dance and theater weren't just creative outlets, but critical survival strategies, mechanisms for building unity and passing down knowledge across generations. In West African societies, for example, drumming and communal dance have long served as a form of storytelling, marking life transitions, honoring ancestors, and strengthening social cohesion. In Aboriginal Australian cultures, the Dreamtime stories—conveyed through dance, song, and visual art—preserve spiritual beliefs and ancestral history, teaching younger generations about land, kinship, and morality. Ancient Greek theater provided a space for civic reflection, allowing citizens to wrestle with questions of justice, power, and human nature through collective emotional experience. These practices weren't extracurricular, despite what Western history classes might have taught us. They were central to how people learned, connected, and made sense of the world.

And yet, somewhere along the way, we've drifted from that collective rhythm. In a society driven by productivity and performance, we often treat these expressions as indulgences rather than necessities, but the hunger for shared experience hasn't gone away—it just shows up differently. It's in the people who sing together at concerts, the strangers who form dance mobs in public squares, the rise of group fitness classes that feel more like community rituals than workouts. We crave those moments when individuality softens into togetherness.

Matteo's hand was a bridge to togetherness. When he moved through the crowd, smiling and playful, he wasn't performing—he was inviting connection. I responded, and I found myself swept into something far more meaningful than a quick dance. I became part of a shared rhythm, a momentary belonging.

Shared experiences break down barriers that words alone can not. They create space for empathy, laughter, and understanding in ways that formal conversation often struggles to achieve. That's part of why I believe so strongly in the power of embodied experience—it speaks to something primal in all of us. When we move together, create together, feel together, it becomes harder to reduce one another to categories, labels, or assumptions.

This truth reflected on a global scale in 2020 during the COVID-19 pandemic. As the world was forced into isolation, we witnessed a resurgence of communal creativity. Across the United States, cities erupted into nightly applause to honor frontline workers. I joined neighbors on the rooftop of my apartment building on West 51st Street and clapped—six feet apart, don't forget—to celebrate the commitment our frontline workers made to care for our community. In Italy, neighbors stood on balconies and sang together. TikTok exploded with dance trends, many created by young people stuck at home who found connection through song and dance. These weren't just moments of entertainment or celebration; they were collective coping mechanisms—ways to reclaim a sense of togetherness when touch, proximity, and routine were stripped away.

When people choose to dance in public, tell their stories through film, or paint a wall that says "Cancel plans, not humanity," they're doing more than creating art; they're breaking the barriers that lead to disconnection. They're reminding us that connection doesn't always begin with words. Sometimes it begins with a rhythm, a glance, or a hand extended across a dancefloor.

Openness isn't just a mindset. It's a practice. When we lean into experiences that stretch us—culturally, emotionally, or even physically—we begin to reclaim the parts of ourselves that fear makes small. We begin to soften our assumptions, expand our understanding, and find meaning in places we never expected to be in.

When I think back to that afternoon in Milan, I don't remember the exact steps I took on the dance floor. I remember how it felt to override the part of me that wanted to hide. I remember how unfamiliar, yet freeing, it felt to choose connection over control—to let someone else lead for a moment and discover that I could trust them enough to follow. That moment cracked me wide open.

Afterward, my body buzzed with electricity that I now realize was aliveness. My heart raced—not with fear, but with exhilaration. I could feel my chest loosen, my breath return to rhythm. As I stepped off the dance floor, I didn't rush to shrink myself again. I let the music echo through me, a quiet reminder of what it felt like to say yes.

Openness doesn't always equate to a grand adventure or dramatic transformation. More often than not, like presence, it's quiet. It's saying *yes* when every instinct screams *no*. It's showing up when you feel awkward or noticing the stories you've been told about who you are and daring to rewrite them. Every time we choose to be open—in the face of fear, discomfort, or uncertainty—we create new possibilities for connection. With others, yes, but also with ourselves.

I'll acknowledge, though, that the world doesn't automatically allow for openness. We are constantly encouraged to perform, to perfect, or to "stay in our lanes." But the moments that shape us, the ones that make us feel fully alive, rarely happen inside our comfort zones. They happen when we loosen our grip. When we step outside of what's expected. When we take someone's hand, unsure of the next step, and move forward anyway.

Openness won't always feel comfortable. That's not the point. Instead, focus on courage. Every time you open yourself—whether it's to a new idea, a new place, or a new version of you—you practice courage. And the more you practice, the easier it becomes to meet the world without armor.

Try this: Think of one small experience you've been avoiding, not out of dislike, but because it feels unfamiliar or uncomfortable. A new class. A daring outfit. A social invite. Write it down, and next to it, jot down what fear or story has held you back. Are you afraid of messing up? Will someone judge you? Do you think you're not good enough?

Now, reframe it. What's the potential joy, growth, or meaning this experience could bring you? Can you hold both the fear and the possibility? Commit to trying one thing this week that invites even a little more openness. And when you do, notice how your body responds. You don't have to feel comfortable. You don't even have to enjoy it. You just have to notice.

Because this is how it starts. With one small yes. One outstretched hand.

I think about how simple Matteo's gesture was, and how much it gave me permission to live differently. The world won't always offer us an invitation so clearly. More often, it will ask us to hold back. But when you feel your instinct pulling you away from connection, remember this: You are allowed to reach toward it anyway.

4

Safety Is a Shared State

L et's start with a feeling.

Imagine yourself in the middle of Times Square. It's early evening. The lights are blinding, flickering against your eyes in every direction. You're shoulder-to-shoulder with strangers, navigating a stream of bodies that never seem to slow.

Close your eyes and imagine you're really there, standing alone in the thick of tourists and professionals, all rushing past you. What do you notice? More importantly, how does your body feel?

There's honking, shouting, music, sirens—your senses are pulled in five directions at once. Your heart beats a little faster. Your breath moves up into your chest. Maybe your jaw tightens without you realizing it. Your body is already reacting.

Now, shift the scene.

Imagine yourself seated in a beach chair on a perfect summer day. The air is warm but not hot. You hear the slow crash of waves. The sky is clear. There's nowhere you need to be, nothing you need to say. No tourists, no noise beyond the repetitive lap of the tide tumbling on the shore. Now what do you notice?

Maybe the feeling of your feet in the sand and the sun on your shoulders. Your breath slows. Your shoulders drop. Your body remembers how to soften.

That contrast? That's your nervous system responding to your environment before a single thought even crosses your mind.

We often think of stress as something internal, something we should be able to manage on our own, but the truth is our surroundings—our spaces, our communities, our relationships—are shaping us constantly. Sometimes they soothe us. Other times they activate our survival instincts.

But what happens when our nervous system adapts so completely to stress that we can no longer tell the difference between safety and survival? When chaos becomes familiar, we stop noticing its impact until it's the only rhythm we know.

The places we exist in and the people we exist with matter. They teach our bodies what's safe and what's not. They shape the way we breathe, how we relate, and our propensity to heal. I've seen this play out in two homes I've visited—neither belonging to people I'm particularly close to, but both left a lasting impression on my nervous system.

River was a friend of someone I once dated. His space was small, a gorgeous studio apartment on the ground floor of a historic brownstone in the heart of Bed-Stuy, but River's character filled the space with warmth—not the building's architecture or its prime Brooklyn location. The lights were dim, the music soft, with friends and family alike propped on the edge of his bed. People came and went without knocking and conversations lingered late into the night. No one ever felt like they had to perform, yet most people in the room were actually Berkley-educated performers.

River's home was the kind of place where your shoulders relaxed the second you stepped inside. Despite the fact that many of his friends had trained at a prestigious music school, there was no posturing, no need to impress. I didn't have to be extraordinary to belong—I just had to be *there*. And when I arrived, I was met with presence and a quiet sense of safety that didn't need to be announced.

Lucy's home told a different story. She was the mother of my first love, and while her hospitality was abundant, it carried weight. Everything was immaculate—napkins coordinated with decorative plates, each dish clearly the product of hours of effort she made certain you knew about, but she shrugged it off by saying, "Oh, it's nothing." The moment I stepped inside, something in my body braced. Lucy was constantly in motion, tidying as guests moved, checking in so often that her attentiveness felt more like tension than comfort.

On the surface, it was a warm welcome, but underneath, my body registered something urgent. Something anxious. A need to control every detail so no one would see the chaos simmering beneath.

Both River and Lucy hoped to make people feel at home, but only one of them succeeded. Lucy left me feeling micromanaged and dysregulated. River created the kind of safety that allowed me to exhale.

This isn't about interior design or good intentions; it's about the nervous system, and—more specifically—co-regulation. Our bodies don't respond to aesthetics; they respond to energy. The subtle cues we give off from the tone of our voice, to the tension in our jaw, or the way we make space (or don't, for that matter), are the signals that communicate to others how safe it is to be near. Warm and regulated subtleties lead others to soften in our presence, whereas sharp and dysregulated behaviors cause them to harden.

Healing doesn't just happen inside of us; it happens between us. And if we want to create the lives and communities that feel grounded and real, we have to learn how to create environments that foster safety for our nervous system—places that don't just look good, but *feel* good, too.

Your Relationships are Rewiring Your Brain

Your nervous system pays attention even when you're on autopilot. It's tracking tone, body language, facial expressions, background noise, lighting, pace, and more. I call this "input." Through experience, it's determining whether the people around you feel safe or unpredictable. That data, paired with your subconscious interpretation of past experiences, tells your body how to respond in real-time via your nervous system.

If you respond positively, you're co-regulating. This is the process by which our nervous systems unconsciously communicate with and influence one another. It's why a calm person can help you feel grounded, or why spending time with someone anxious can leave you feeling drained, even if nothing "bad" happened. Sidebar—I call these people *energy vampires*.

Here's the important part: The more consistently your body is exposed to a particular environment, the more familiar it becomes. If your system is regularly activated by chaos, criticism, pressure, or unpredictability, your brain starts to normalize those cues. Hypervigilance becomes your baseline. There's a rhythm to stress despite its unpredictability.

On the other hand, when your body consistently encounters calm, compassion, and care, those signals begin to rewrite your internal map of safety. This is where neuroplasticity comes in.

Neuroplasticity is the brain's ability to reorganize itself, forming new neural connections and pruning old ones in response to experience. In simple terms, your brain adapts to what it's repeatedly exposed to, and that includes your relationships.

For people who grew up in emotionally unpredictable homes, this can feel especially significant. Their baseline may be anxious, even in relationships that aren't threatening. They may over-accommodate, avoid conflict, or constantly monitor others' moods because their nervous system has been trained to equate closeness with caution, but when they enter relationships that feel safe—where boundaries are respected and emotions are regulated—healing can begin. Not instantly, and not without effort, but slowly, their nervous system learns that it doesn't have to brace for impact anymore.

That's the beauty of co-regulation. It reminds us that healing doesn't happen in isolation—it occurs in community through consistent exposure to safe, warm, and attuned people. Though it's important to note that the inverse is true, too. Environments that are aesthetically curated but emotionally rigid, like Lucy's home, may offer hospitality, but not true connection. A home may be filled with nice things, but if the energy feels tense, on edge, or performative, it's often interpreted as unsafe. Safety isn't about how something looks, but how it feels.

The Architecture of Belonging

It's easy to think of "space" as purely physical, but our environments are shaped just as much by energy and emotional tone as they are by furniture and lighting. The question isn't just "What does this room look like?" but "How does it feel to exist in this room?"

Whether it's a home, an office, or a gathering of friends, the spaces we fill and the people we fill them with can either soothe our nervous systems or quietly stress them. You have more influence than you may think, though. You can choose to design your environment—internally and externally—with intention.

Here are a few strategies that foster emotional safety and genuine connection:

1. Lead with Regulation, Not Perfection

The most comforting people aren't the ones who say all the right things; they're the ones who feel calm in their own bodies. Your presence matters more than your words. If you want to help someone feel at ease, tend to your own nervous system first. Breathe slowly. Speak gently. Hold eye contact. Make space for silence. Then watch how your energy ripples outward.

There's an unmistakable aura around someone who is grounded. Their presence feels like an exhale. You find yourself slowing down—not because they ask you to, but because your body instinctively mirrors theirs. They aren't trying to manage the room or make everything feel comfortable. They're just there, calm, steady, and regulated. And that kind of energy is contagious.

2. **Prioritize Comfort Over Performance**

The spaces that make us feel most at home aren't the ones that look perfect, but the ones that feel calm. Environments where your body softens without you having to think about it. Over time, as people begin to heal and learn to regulate their own nervous systems, overstimulation starts to feel like a threat. Bright lights, chaotic energy, loud environments, or hosts who appear fragile beneath the surface—it all becomes harder to ignore.

Consciousness, though, makes it difficult to exist in dysregulated spaces. Once your body knows peace, it can't un-know it. The chaos that once felt normal starts to feel like a warning sign.

I witness this shift in my clients often. As they begin to regulate their internal worlds, they become more protective of their external ones. Spaces that once felt exciting start to feel overwhelming. Relationships that were once stimulating gradually become more exhausting. And slowly, people begin to crave something different—something easy, quiet, and safe.

This craving is cultural. In recent years, there's been a noticeable return to structure, simplicity, and tradition in various forms. Think of the rise of "trad wife" aesthetics running wild on social media, or the resurgence of interest in organized religion and spiritual communities, not always for their doctrines, but for the predictability and ritual they offer. For many, these frameworks don't just represent values—they offer a balm for the nervous system. Something to take the edge off of reality. A sense of rhythm. A belief that someone or something is in control, so they can let go. And in a world that feels increasingly chaotic, the escape is incredibly grounding.

Even people who don't resonate with certain belief systems may find comfort in their rituals—lighting candles on Fridays, gathering on Sundays, kneeling in prayer, cooking from scratch. These patterns regulate us. They provide containers for community, clarity in routine, and a simple structure the modern world rarely allows for.

It's easy to write these cultural norms off as outdated or overly simplistic, but their appeal is often rooted in something deeper: the longing for safety, predictability, and connection. And we're seeing it reflected across the nation. According to a 2023-2024 Pew Research Center study, around 62% of U.S. adults still identify as Christian—a figure that, despite decades of gradual decline, has stabilized in recent years. Interestingly, Gen Z is showing a renewed curiosity in religious or spiritual practices, not necessarily out of doctrinal commitment, but out of a desire for structure, meaning, and shared experience.

It's not surprising, considering the United States just experienced one of the most turbulent elections in American history in 2024. The turbulence started, for the most part, with President Trump's first term in 2017. It escalated during the COVID-19 pandemic, and again when President Trump ran for re-election in 2024. It's natural that people would search for peace amidst sociopolitical chaos.

But community isn't limited to formal religious or spiritual spaces—it also shows up in the moments people mobilize to meet each other's needs. Following natural disasters like Hurricane Katrina, the Los Angeles wildfires, or even the early days of the COVID-19 pandemic, it is often grassroots initiatives—not top-down systems—that provide the most immediate support.

Food drives, neighborhood shelters, and mutual aid networks are relational responses (in addition to logistical next steps following disaster). Between the lines, these responses say: *I see you. You're not alone.*

In this type of community, structure doesn't always look like a Sunday sermon or a perfectly set table. Sometimes it looks like bags of clothes, canned vegetables, and a human chain to rescue someone from floodwaters. And sometimes, when we're lucky, it looks like shared laughter around a potluck table in a community center. Or folding chairs, a table, and a deck of cards in a garage, if you grew up like I did.

In the end, it's not just the rules or the rituals that comfort us. It's the co-regulation that happens when people gather with a shared purpose. The rhythm of collective care. The sense that someone else is there, holding part of the weight with you.

That's why comfort matters more than performance. Forget the curated aesthetic or the spotless kitchen. True connection lives in the feeling that nothing is required of you. That you're welcome to breathe, take up space, and exist without pretense. Soften the lighting. Choose cozy seating. Minimize noise. Let go of perfection. A calm space doesn't just soothe the nervous system; it invites people to stay.

3. **Remember Where You Come From**

I didn't always have the language for nervous system regulation or co-regulation, but I knew the feeling of safety when I experienced it.

I was raised Catholic. If you know anything about Catholicism, you know the religion itself wasn't the "safe" part, but the rituals and routines often were. Sundays were routine—church, drawn-out sermons that should have been cut short, and, if we were lucky, breakfast at the diner after mass. The diner was always packed with "church people," as I called them. Familiar faces I never truly knew the names of, lingering conversations, and the clink of coffee cups. It wasn't glamorous, but it felt like belonging, even if it was belonging by proximity, not intimacy. We weren't sharing our souls, but we were sharing space—breathing the same air, nodding in quiet recognition, and anchoring ourselves to the same weekly rhythm. And somehow, that was enough.

On the opposite end of the intimacy spectrum, Friday

nights were often reserved for family. I loved going to my godmother's house, where the adults sat around the table talking late into the night. I'd try to keep up, even when the conversation moved too fast or flew over my head. Sometimes my uncle smoked cigarettes inside—I remember thinking it looked cool in a way that only kids growing up in the 90s could find cool. But what really stuck with me wasn't the cigarettes, though the smoke certainly tried, but the feeling that I was part of something bigger than myself. That I didn't have to earn my place because I was already welcomed.

Back then, I recognized two truths about community, even if I couldn't articulate it at the time: Community could be structured and ritualistic, like Sunday service, or messy and impromptu, like cigarettes and cards at the dining room table. I also learned that safety wasn't about silence or control. It was presence. Familiarity. Being with people who let you show up exactly as you are.

As I got older, I found new rituals in new places. Friday night football games as captain of the cheerleading team. Late-night drives to sit by the river with friends. One of my best friends, Eric, still lives in our hometown. We've been friends for nearly fifteen years. Every time I visit, I ask for "backyard beers." Not because I care to sip Bud Light at the age of thirty, but because of what those nights represent. Some of our best memories were made in lawn chairs, drinking cheap beer under string lights or stars. There's no agenda, no pressure to entertain—just a rhythm we both fall into in lockstep.

That's the thing about community—it doesn't have to be big, or loud, or even organized. It just has to be real.

When I talk to clients about healing in community, I'm not asking them to join a church or start hosting dinner parties. I'm inviting them to notice how they feel in the spaces they already occupy. To pay attention to people who allow their shoulders to drop. To create routines that feel grounding, even if they're as simple as Sunday coffee with a friend or a standing dinner with chosen family.

Close your eyes and recall a moment when you felt safe with others. Not just mentally safe, but physically at ease. Maybe it was a group dinner, a porch conversation, or a moment of laughter with friends.

Let your body remember what it was like to be there.

What did you hear? What did the air smell like? How did your breath feel? Notice what happens in your body as you recall it. Let that memory settle into your nervous system like a rhythm you can return to at any time.

The Space Between Us

When we feel safe, we heal. When we are seen, we soften. When we build spaces that invite presence, spaces where performance is replaced with ease, we take care of each other.

Before we close out the chapter, take a moment to check in with your body. How do you feel right now? Not just mentally, but physically. Is your breath a little slower? Are your shoulders more relaxed? That feeling, if it's there, isn't just yours. It's *ours*.

The stories I shared in this chapter—of River's home, of communal rituals, of backyard beers and Sundays at the diner—carry energy that soothes. Energy that communicates, "You're safe here." But that peace? It's not just coming from within you. It's *my* energy that you're feeling. *My* nervous system, *my* calm, *my* stories. This is co-regulation in action—through words and connections that transcend pages.

And as much as I'd love to preserve this feeling—to bottle it up and hand it to you as permanent refuge, though I'd likely be out of a job if that were the case—I want to take you back, just for a moment, to Times Square. Remember the rush? The noise? The tightness in your chest? That was your body, too. And that contrast matters.

Healing doesn't happen in isolation. It occurs in motion, in the shifts between chaos and calm, between disconnection and presence. The goal isn't to escape the world, but to return to it more rooted and anchored in peace. To recognize the moments when your body braces and to seek out the people and places where it softens.

We're told healing is an inside job, but co-regulation tells the truth: Safety is a shared state. You don't have to find your safety alone. You don't have to "heal" or "love yourself" to prepare for a deep and fulfilling relationship. You just have to be human, flowing with the rhythm of your nervous system. Let your nervous system lead you. I promise it knows the way.

5

The Process of Unlearning

Question: What if the problem was never you?

Hear me out.

What if the anxiety you carry isn't a personal flaw, but a learned response to unpredictability? What if the guilt you feel when setting a boundary was taught to you by people who benefited from your passivity? What if the reason you tolerate chaos is because your nervous system learned that love and pain were often in the same room?

We don't come into this world knowing how to betray ourselves—we're taught.

We learn to self-sacrifice in relationships when care is conditional.

We learn to silence ourselves in systems that punish vulnerability.

We learn to abandon our needs in environments that praise perfection.

And yet, most of us go on blaming *ourselves* for the messes we were handed.

This chapter is personal. It includes stories about abuse, trauma, and suicide. There will be pain—but also truth, healing, and bits of dark humor. Because sometimes, that's how we learn to survive.

For now, we'll talk about unlearning: Unlearning is the slow, messy process of putting those pieces down that are no longer ours to carry. It's what happens when we stop asking, *"What's wrong with me?"* and start asking, *"Who taught me to think this way?"* Unlearning happens when we stop confusing suffering with strength, silence with maturity, and proximity with love. That process doesn't start with fixing yourself. It starts with telling the truth about the systems, relationships, and beliefs that shaped you.

It starts right here, right now. And it's a radical reclaiming of truth in a world that conditions us to forget who we are.

If asked, I imagine Brandon didn't grow up calling what he experienced "abusive." He'd probably call it a hard childhood. I can't ask him, though, because he's dead.

He often said things like, "My dad just had a temper," or "My mom did the best she could." Both were true. But for most of his short life, he didn't question the pain—he normalized it. Until he died by suicide at the age of twenty.

When Brandon and I first met, we created a relationship that mirrored ones we both witnessed growing up: raised voices, items thrown across the room, threats of suicide, abandonment, and more. We both equated love with intensity. Highs and lows. I didn't realize then that I was replicating what I had seen in my own household—or what he saw in his—until it was over.

When he raised a concern, I shut down. When I needed space, he took it personally. And when either of us felt overwhelmed or hurt, we didn't know how to soothe ourselves, so we reacted instead. Loudly. Emotionally. Sometimes with words that left marks. I didn't throw things, but I remember slamming doors, raising my voice, and retreating into silence for hours. I wasn't trying to hurt him. I truly believe that he wasn't trying to hurt me, either. We both just wanted to feel heard. What we didn't understand back then was that when pain speaks unchecked, it echoes.

Both of us stayed longer than we should have. I tried to reason with him. To help him see how his reactions were impacting me, but he wasn't ready to hear it—not because he didn't care, but because he hadn't "done the work" yet. Nor could he, to be fair. Brandon supported his family with the paychecks he received after exhausting days of blue-collar labor. He didn't have time, let alone energy, to heal.

I was tired, too. I was battling my own family system at home. Every argument with my parents felt layered—like I wasn't just fighting them, but Brandon, too. Even the ghosts of my past. Every slammed door, raised voice, and desperate apology carried the weight of generations. Neither of us had the tools to break the cycle back then; we only had the patterns we were taught: survive, lash out, cling harder. We mistook chaos for connection because it was the only map we were given.

The Systems We Inherit

Our personal relationships don't exist in a vacuum. They are shaped by the larger systems we're born into—systems that often reward domination over cooperation, obedience over curiosity, survival over connection. Poverty, racism, classism, ableism, homophobia, police brutality. These aren't just buzzwords or political talking points; they're lived realities that train nervous systems to operate in survival mode, or "fight or flight," as we therapists like to call it. When you grow up fighting to exist inside systems that punish your very being, it becomes almost impossible to differentiate love from survival.

Trauma researchers call this "betrayal trauma"—the wounds that occur when the very people or institutions meant to protect you become a source of harm. And once betrayal becomes familiar, it's hard to trust safety when you find it (Freyd, 1996; 2008). Abuse isn't just relational. It's systemic. It's baked into how housing policies are written, how policing is conducted, how healthcare is accessed (or denied), and how education is funded.

In these systems, we learn fear before we learn trust.

We learn scarcity before abundance.

Defense before vulnerability.

And that learning seeps into our bodies, our relationships, our communities—until it feels like "just the way things are." And trust that I know how naive this sounds coming from a white woman who grew up in the suburbs of New Jersey. If I could change the reality of the world, I would. But one person alone is not capable of global change, despite how often motivational speakers will try to convince you otherwise.

True and sustainable systemic change forces us to be realistic. I often say to clients, "You don't get to choose the systems, but you're forced to participate in them, so let's figure out how to manage in the meantime."

Where the Macro (Systems) Meets the Micro (Self)

And like so many who lived in pain and chaos for too long without the tools to survive, Brandon eventually gave up.

It didn't happen overnight, nor were we together when it did. Over time, the weight of carrying everyone—his parents, his siblings, the expectations he could never meet, and the lows of our relationship, if I'm being honest—wore him down. Then the unthinkable happened.

Through hearsay, I learned his brother was the one to find his body. As a human, my heart aches for him. But as a therapist,

I fear the life-long imprint that discovery left on his brother's nervous system.

At the time, I felt abandoned. I ran through questions like *how could he leave me here?* And *what am I supposed to do now?* In hindsight, I see that Brandon's death was the beginning of my unlearning. When someone holds up a mirror to the darkness within, you can either shatter the mirror or take a long, hard look at yourself.

I did both.

Eric called to tell me about Brandon's death. I was living in Italy at the time. It was late, so I stepped outside on the balcony overlooking Corso Sempione and Arco della Pace in Milan so as not to disturb my host family, who were all sound asleep. Eric asked me to sit down. Softly, he said, "Brandon is dead." Then we sat in silence for at least ten minutes until he was brave enough to break the silence with, "Are you OK?"

"Yes," I replied. To this day, I don't think I lied.

It's an odd thing when your abuser commits suicide. I'd be lying if I said I wasn't a little relieved. *He can never hurt me again,* I thought. That was true. But I was also devastated. I didn't come to understand that devastation for a few more years, when I finally let myself heal.

Like some heartbroken humans, I started running, both emotionally and physically. I liked the silence and the sound of my feet hitting the pavement. I chased the adrenaline and the dopamine with every new benchmark. My first fifteen miles were simultaneously my worst and my best, much like my heart-break. It was no different than the emotional rollercoaster I'd experienced after Brandon's death—relief at first, thinking, *It's not so bad*, followed by a bumpy ride of ups and downs that make you question if you'll ever make it out alive, all amounting to an accomplishment that drowns out the struggle. A few years later, after I moved to New York, I hit fifteen miles again. Those miles felt effortless.

By then, I had squeezed almost everything I possibly could have out of running. I ran half marathons and proudly displayed the medals on my wall. Running also gave me the time and space to process my abusive relationship, placing one foot after another while always moving forward. It made me feel *good*. I felt alive for the first time in years. After my abusive relationship, I often questioned if I was dead inside. Running brought me back to life.

It also brought me back to Brandon, in some sick and twisted way. I hold less resentment and anger towards my abusive ex than I do others. In fact, I love him. I really, truly do. They say grief isn't a matter of moving forward, but learning to live with it. I created so much space in my heart for Brandon that I actually feel empathetic towards him.

Now, don't get me wrong—I'm not excusing Brandon's behavior. Abusing me was wrong. But if I really look in the mirror, I know I abused him, too. It feels weird to put that in writing.

I'm sitting in seat 4A on a United flight from Newark to San Diego as I type. I'm surrounded by strangers who know nothing about me, and yet I am writing about one of the most profound and hurtful chapters of my life. I'm sharing my ugly, naked truths to no one but myself, and everyone around me is just . . . here.

But something beautiful happens when you confront the worst parts of yourself. You learn to feel all of it, and you look at the world differently. Now, I sit next to strangers, and I lead with kindness and empathy. I smile at the people around me. I make small talk with the flight attendants. Most importantly, I hold my head high—not because my story is perfect, but because I believe, even still, that people are inherently good. It's the environments we're shaped by—the pain, the scarcity, the fear—that sometimes pull us away from that goodness.

Unlearning at Scale

The 2020 Black Lives Matter protests reminded the world that people *want* to do better. Millions of people took to the streets to protest individual acts of violence while demanding a reckoning with the systems that produce that violence. The marches, the chants, the community bail funds, the mutual aid groups—they were all acts of unlearning. A refusal to accept injustice as inevitable. A collective reminder that systems can and *should* be challenged, but unless we organize, they'll never be rewritten, our greatest systemic limitation.

I often think about the social and emotional barriers to systemic change—fear, discomfort, a general "walking on eggshells" type feeling—and I can't help but notice how often we remain stuck, not because change is impossible, but because we're too afraid of offending someone along the way. We fear saying the wrong thing, asking the wrong question, or being perceived as ignorant. As a result, we've collectively become hypersensitive to hurt.

Instead of taking the risk, we say nothing. Then we're judged by people who claim, "Silence is compliance," which just paralyzes us more. They're right, but it's not helping the situation—it's just furthering the divide between the privileged and the oppressed.

This dance, often hostile and violent, creates a new form of classism, one defined by social and emotional hierarchy. Those who know the "right" language, the "right" movements, and the "right" causes stand atop a fragile pedestal, while those still learning—or simply afraid of getting it wrong—are pushed further into silence and shame. We say we want change, but too often, we punish people for not having arrived there fast enough.

What we forget is that unlearning, by its very nature, is messy. It requires room for mistakes and vulnerable questions. It demands humility on both sides—the humility to admit when we've caused harm and the humility to accept an imperfect apology as part of a larger process. Real healing and progress doesn't happen by shaming people into submission. It needs space to stumble, to reflect, and to choose differently.

In fact, repair is what makes relationships stronger, both personally and collectively. We cannot create a culture of accountability without simultaneously creating a culture of compassion. Without it, we're not inviting people into growth; we're scaring them away from it.

The truth is, the systems that harm us are fueled by disconnection. By fear. By people "staying in their lanes," "walking on eggshells," too afraid to reach across the divide. If we want something different, we have to be willing to risk discomfort in favor of repair. We have to normalize doing it badly at first and trusting that repair—true, earnest repair—builds trust in people and places where none existed before.

Because as long as fear rules the process, the cycle of pain will continue. As long as we're more invested in being "right" or "politically correct" than being real, the walls between us will only grow higher. Unlearning invites a different path. A messier, braver, and more compassionate path.

It invites us to step toward the conversations we're afraid to have. To listen when it's easier to defend. To correct with kindness instead of condemnation. To reach for repair, not perfection. It invites us to tell the truth about the systems we were born into—not with the goal of absolving ourselves, but with the goal of dismantling the parts of those systems that live within us.

Because if pain can be taught, healing can be taught, too.

And the work of unlearning—of breaking generational cycles, challenging systemic oppression, or forging healthier ways of relating to ourselves and others—begins not with mastery, but with a simple, radical decision to stay open and willing. The goal is to keep reaching for each other, even when it's hard.

From Survival to Self-Trust

My abusive relationship wore me down until I had nothing left. And in the emptiness, I found softness. Accountability. A deep desire to be someone I could trust. Not just in love, but in every room I walk into. Unlearning isn't about perfection; it's about ownership. It's telling the truth—not just about what happened to you, but about who you became in response, and who you want to be next.

If pain can be taught, healing can be taught, too.

That's the promise of unlearning: We aren't doomed to repeat the patterns we inherited. But unlearning isn't clean. It's not a twelve-step program or a linear ascent from wounded to wise. It's a messy, circular journey of noticing, grieving, choosing differently, and sometimes failing before choosing differently again. It requires a level of honesty that most of us aren't prepared for at first. Not just honesty about the people who hurt us, but about the ways we participated once we learned the "rules." We replicate what we think is normal until something (or someone) shows us there's another way.

Sometimes that "something" is heartbreak. Or worse, the death of someone who broke your heart. Sometimes it's exhaustion. Other times it's a whisper so soft we almost miss it, telling us, *This doesn't have to be your life.* Unlearning asks us to step out of survival mode and into a space where reflection is possible. To recognize that self-betrayal wasn't a flaw, it was a strategy. It asks us to understand that silence, people-pleasing, self-abandonment, perfectionism, even rage—they were all strangers, born from environments that didn't allow for safe options.

In short: We do what we have to do to survive. I say that a lot in therapy with clients. But when you start to unlearn, survival isn't enough. Now, you're invested in living *differently.*

So I'll ask again: What if the problem was never you?

Maybe you're starting to see what I mean.

Maybe the anxiety you carry was never yours to begin with. Maybe the guilt, the perfectionism, the self-abandonment—maybe they were taught to you by environments that demanded survival, not authenticity. And maybe unlearning isn't about becoming someone new, but finally returning to the person you were before the world taught you to be afraid.

The process of unlearning is painful because it asks us to sit in discomfort. It asks us to tell the truth. It demands that we look in the mirror and stop apologizing for who we became while trying to survive, and instead, start choosing differently, even when it's hard. Even when it means losing people who were only ever committed to the older version of us.

But unlearning isn't where the story ends. No, this is just the beginning.

The next step is remembering who you are underneath all of it, and learning to trust that person enough to build a life, a community, and a future that doesn't just heal you, but helps heal the spaces you touch. And it all starts with radical curiosity. Curiosity isn't just the beginning of personal healing; it's the foundation for collective transformation.

Unlearning in Action

Unlearning starts with remembering: You didn't invent these patterns; you inherited them. They were shaped by family norms, cultural scripts, and systems that reward self-abandonment over self-trust.

When you catch yourself repeating an old pattern, pause before self-blame. Ask: *Who taught me this? What system benefits when I keep doing it?* That awareness is the crack in the foundation that leads to unlearning.

Here are some common patterns and the systems they're tied to:

1. **Staying in unhealthy or toxic relationships** - a legacy of intergenerational trauma that normalizes chaos, control, or neglect as "love."

   To overcome: Learn healthy relationship dynamics. Read books like *Attached* by Amir Levine and Rachel S. F. Heller or *Emotional Inheritance* by Galit Atlas. Go to therapy. There are a variety of resources, many of them free, that are accessible to you *now*. Don't wait to start the process of unlearning.

2. **Overworking or tying your worth to productivity** - the conditioning of capitalism, where exhaustion and burnout are benchmarks for achievement.

   To overcome: Find a healthy work/life balance. If your current job doesn't allow for balance, find a new one. Learn to create boundaries at   work so you're not available 24/7, even if it's just one to two hours for yourself in the morning before hopping online. Journal about the   connection between your self-worth and productivity. Explore shadow work. Do one thing differently *now*, master it, then build from there. In two years, you'll have a radically different relationship with work (and with yourself).

3. **Playing it "safe" and avoiding risks that could elevate your financial standing** - a survival skill shaped by poverty, where stability feels safer than risking loss for potential gain.

   To overcome: Build financial literacy. Read books like *The Psychology of Money* by Morgan Housel. Follow content creators who will teach you about simple investment and retirement strategies. Spend one to two hours per week learning the skills your parents and grandparents weren't fortunate enough to develop. Generational wealth starts with *you*.

4. **Avoiding conflict at all costs** - often rooted in family systems that punished vulnerability and rewarded compliance.

   To overcome: Desensitize to conflict. Tell your friends and family openly that you're learning to stand up for yourself and share your opinion, then *do* it. When you feel like you want to run away, run toward it. Lead with, "This is hard for me, but it's important I talk about it, so please bear with me." Go to therapy to explore your conflict avoidance. Journal about conflicts you've avoided in the past, what you could have done differently, and the barriers you might have faced.

5. **Ignoring your own needs to keep others comfortable** - reinforced by gender norms and cultures that equate selflessness with virtue.

To overcome: Reflect on the roles and responsibilities you were raised to follow. Connect the dots between past and present—*how do these childhood norms show up in adulthood?* Explore what you could do differently in the present day. Remind yourself that you have free will. Learn how to set and maintain boundaries. Challenge the beliefs that prevent you from setting boundaries.

These patterns didn't start with you, but they can end with you. Unlearning isn't about fixing everything at once—it's about noticing the script you've been handed and choosing to rewrite it one line at a time. Every time you challenge one of these inherited ways of being, you loosen the grip of the systems that shaped them. You create a little more space for freedom, for connection, for a life that's truly *yours.* And with each choice, no matter how small, you're proving to yourself that change is possible. That's where unlearning begins.

6

Foster Awareness Through Curiosity

Healing begins when you start asking better questions, or at least that's what Sam taught me.

We met in Patagonia after a long day of hiking and horseback riding through the mountains of El Chaltén. We were strangers, paired together by chance over wine and steak as the sun disappeared behind the peaks. What started as small talk quickly deepened into a conversation about the kind of life change you can feel taking shape before you can even name it.

Sam was the type of person who didn't shy away from the real questions—within minutes, we were unpacking endings and exploring new beginnings. We spoke candidly about how sometimes the bravest thing you can do is admit that the life you worked so hard to build no longer fits and make a change. She told me about the life she was walking away from: a secure job in corporate America, the type of job you're supposed to want. On paper, it was everything—stability, prestige, a clear path laid out neatly in front of her. But somewhere along the way, it stopped feeling like *her*. So she chose to step off the path without knowing exactly where the next one leads, and it happened to land her in Patagonia, across the table from an equally lost therapist (me).

I told Sam about the life I was trying to build. About leaving behind a relationship that no longer fit and the loud, gut-wrenching grief that followed. About venturing into private practice, where every day felt like both a risk and a reclamation. I was still so close to the ending that I couldn't quite see the beginning yet.

There was no need for performance between us. No pressure to make our lives sound prettier or more certain than they were. We sat there, shadows flickering across our faces from the open flame of the asado—an Argentine style of communal barbeque—suspended in our own separate, but strangely parallel, liminal spaces, allowing the unknown to be what it was. Uncomfortable, scary, and strangely hopeful.

Somewhere between the wine and the steak, Sam said something I'll never forget: "It's not about finding the right answers. It's about asking better questions." I knew exactly what she meant.

Curiosity isn't just a mindset—it's a posture. A willingness to look again, ask deeper questions, and hold space for what we don't know just yet. It softens our defenses and makes it possible to explore our inner world without judgment. Where shame closes the door, curiosity cracks it open and says, "There's more to this story."

In the wake of unlearning, curiosity becomes the next necessary step. Once you've dismantled the stories that shaped you, you're left with the question, "Now what?" You've questioned your conditioning and begun to let go of survival-based patterns, but healing isn't just about shedding. It's about discovery. Expansion. Reclaiming the parts of yourself that never got a chance to speak.

Curiosity is active. It invites us to sit with uncertainty, to follow the threads of our own stories, and to approach our past with compassion rather than critique. Where judgment asks, "What's wrong with me?" curiosity gently asks, "What happened to me?" and "What is possible now?" The goal isn't to arrive at some definitive truth, but to remain open to what's unfolding. That openness—that willingness to stay in the questions—is where transformation begins.

In therapy, I often encourage clients to get curious about their reactions instead of rushing to fix them.

What does that part of you need right now?

Where did you learn that?

What would it feel like to choose differently?

These questions don't offer quick answers, but they create room for movement—movement toward awareness, empathy, and change. Because let's be honest: Answers can be comforting, but they can also be limiting. Answers imply closure. Curiosity, on the other hand, keeps us in relationship—with ourselves, with others, and with the evolving nature of what it means to heal. It shifts us from control to connection, from fear to possibility. And in a world that constantly demands certainty, choosing curiosity—much like openness, as we discussed in Chapter Three—is a radical act.

Sam's question stayed with me long after Patagonia. I think about it often, particularly when I sit across from clients who feel lost, or when I catch myself trying to figure out my "next best step." I simply remind myself: *Ask better questions.*

So let me ask you this: What might shift if, instead of needing certainty, you allowed space for exploration? What if not knowing didn't mean you were failing, but evolving? This is the heart of healing. Not answers, but awareness. Not certainty, but curiosity.

Curiosity, practiced consistently, becomes a form of emotional resilience. It keeps us in conversation with the parts of ourselves we don't fully understand yet. When we ask, "Why do I shut down in conflict?" or "When did I learn to confuse safety with silence?", we open doors that shame would rather keep closed.

It doesn't demand immediate answers or pressure us to solve everything at once. Curiosity gives us permission to pause, reflect, and hold complexity without rushing to label things as right or wrong. It shifts us from self-criticism to self-compassion, marked by a full-body sigh or a clenched jaw releasing. That's often where healing begins.

Curiosity also transforms how we relate to others. It makes space for misunderstanding without rupture, invites openness in conflict, and interrupts patterns of disconnection. We listen to understand, not just to respond. We ask, "What made you feel that way?" instead of placing blame.

Curiosity isn't about tolerating harm—it's about gathering information before drawing conclusions. In a culture obsessed with certainty, it's a radical practice. It invites patience, deepens intimacy, and creates connection in a world that often rewards division over understanding.

This matters deeply in activist and justice-centered spaces, too. When we only value perfection, we lose people who are trying to learn. Performative allyship—saying the right words, sharing the right posts, adopting the right vocabulary—becomes a shield for image maintenance, not a tool for transformation. And "cancel culture," for all its roots in accountability, can sometimes replicate the very systems of shame it seeks to dismantle.

Curiosity doesn't require you to excuse harm. Instead, it asks, "What made this person believe that harm was acceptable? What systems taught them that? What conditions allowed it to persist?" These questions don't minimize responsibility; they deepen it. If we want real change, we have to understand how beliefs are formed and how they can be *re*formed.

In moments of global crisis—when the world feels like it's unraveling—curiosity becomes a spiritual practice. Existential questioning is how we navigate chaos. It's how we turn grief into meaning and despair into movement. Whether we're wrestling with climate crisis, genocide, political extremism, mass deportation, or the erosion of truth itself, the question beneath all others remains the same: *What kind of world do we want to create, and who must we become to build it?*

I think about the summer of 2020 a lot. The protests, the public reckonings, the black squares on Instagram that seemed to multiply overnight. I lived on Sullivan and Bleecker, just two blocks south of Washington Square Park in New York City, one of the largest meeting points for demonstrators following the murder of George Floyd on May 25, 2020. According to the New York Times (2020), an estimated 500,000 people participated in demonstrations across the U.S. as part of the Black Lives Matter movement. For a brief moment, it felt like the world had cracked open.

People were marching, questioning, unlearning. Books like *White Fragility* and *How to Be Antiracist* were sold out everywhere. There was a collective hunger for change, but also a quiet panic beneath it. People didn't want to be wrong. They didn't want to be seen as complicit. So they performed correctness instead of leaning into transformation.

Friends and strangers alike posted black squares. Businesses pushed diversity, equity, and inclusion (DEI). Influencers made statements. People were having long-overdue conversations. But beneath it all, many were asking the wrong question, like, "How do I not get called out?", when the questions should have been, "What have I ignored? Whose pain have I avoided, and why?"

Curiosity was largely absent in those moments—not because people didn't care, but because shame took the lead. Shame shuts down the very reflection that growth requires. It punishes people for not knowing instead of encouraging them to keep asking.

But when we lead with curiosity instead of shame, we create space for people to stay. We let discomfort serve a purpose. We teach that accountability is possible without public humiliation or confrontation, and that allyship is a daily practice, not a performance.

Because that moment in history wasn't just about justice, it was about identity. About asking, "Who am I in relation to this harm?" "What do I believe?" and "Where do I need to listen to more closely?" These are existential questions, not checklist items. And they can't be answered by reposting a quote or reading one book about anti-racism. They require a lifelong posture of humility—one that says, "I know I will never fully arrive, but I will keep showing up anyway."

I once worked with a client—I'll call her Ana—who came to therapy deeply conflicted. She grew up in a politically conservative household, but had recently begun to explore more progressive values. The dissonance between who she had been raised to be and who she was becoming left her feeling stuck between worlds. In session, she'd say things like, "I feel like I'm betraying my family," and "What if I'm wrong?"

At first, Ana approached her evolution like a test—searching for the right answer, trying to land on a singular identity that would make the inner tension go away. But what she eventually discovered was that healing didn't come from choosing a side. It came from staying curious and asking questions like, "Why did I believe that?" or "Who taught me that was true?"

Through our work, Ana didn't just shift her beliefs—she softened. She began to see that her upbringing wasn't inherently "bad" or "good," it was simply incomplete. She could love her family *and* challenge the worldview they gave her. She could feel grief for her past *and* still move forward. Her growth didn't require her to disown her story, but to expand it.

That's what curiosity does. It doesn't ask you to discard your history. It asks you to hold it with context and compassion, and then decide if it still fits.

Progressive values, at their core, aren't just about being "liberal" or politically left-leaning—they're about one's willingness to question the status quo. According to Merriam-Webster (2025), progressivism is a political philosophy and social reform movement focused on advancing the public good through government action. It stems from a deep curiosity about how things came to be and whether they still serve us.

Curiosity asks, "Who benefits from this system, and who gets left out?" for the purpose of "What might be possible if we did things differently?"

This is why curiosity and empathy are inseparable. When we stay curious about someone's experience—especially when it differs from our own—we create space for connection. We don't have to agree to understand. We don't have to share someone's story to care about its outcome. But we do have to be willing to listen without rushing to correct, debate, or defend.

Empathy without curiosity becomes performative. Curiosity without empathy becomes voyeurism. But together? They're a force for change. They challenge us to sit with nuance. To resist easy answers. To move beyond "us versus them" and into "What's true for you, and how can I hold that alongside what's true for me?"

That's why this inner work—the softening, the questioning, the expanding—isn't just personal, it's political. It's relational. And it's *urgently* needed. Because this kind of work—the work of staying open when it would be easier to shut down—mirrors what's needed on a global scale.

The world is in a collective identity crisis. Institutions are breaking down. Climate disasters are increasing. Trust in governments, media, and public systems is eroding. And amid all this upheaval, we're being asked to reimagine nearly everything: what safety means, what justice looks like, how we care for each other, and what it means to be human in a fractured world.

It's no wonder so many of us feel overwhelmed, but overwhelm isn't a reason to disengage—it's a call to get curious. Because when we ask better questions, we don't just change our own lives, we create ripples outward. We influence our relationships, our communities, and the systems we're a part of. We begin to challenge the binaries—this or that, right or wrong, good or bad—and, instead, begin to ask, "What if both are true?" or "What am I not seeing yet?"

This is the work of healing in the collective. It doesn't happen through outrage alone, but through inquiry. Nuance. Brave conversations and uncomfortable truths. Through remembering that the point isn't to arrive at a final, fixed answer—it's to keep learning, listening, and choosing curiosity, even when it would be easier to shut down.

And just like that night in Patagonia, when Sam and I sat across from each other sharing stories of endings and beginnings, we return to the same essential truth: The questions matter more than the answers. Because the answers will change as you do, but the courage to keep asking, to keep listening, to keep showing up with an open heart, will change *you*—and maybe the world—forever.

7

Understand Resistance and Redefine Success

The American dream is a lie.

We're told that if we work hard, get good grades, and follow the rules, success will follow. Stability will be achieved. Respect will be earned. You might even be happy. But what no one dares to say out loud is that the system you are trying to succeed in wasn't built with your well-being in mind. It was built to keep you striving, producing, achieving—and quietly burning out.

The lie isn't that success is possible; it's that it's equally accessible. For the wealthy and the white—the people these systems were built for—success isn't a dream, it's a blueprint. For everyone else, it's a miracle. But now our systems are so polarized and our economy so unpredictable that even those with privilege are starting to notice the fallacies of the American dream.

I was in the thick of graduate school, consulting with a professor I admired most about whether I should continue in academia and pursue a Ph.D. He didn't hesitate.

"Don't do it," Dr. Abrams said, smiling with a kind of knowing warmth. "You don't need more school to do something meaningful. Academia will try to convince you otherwise, but you can change lives without the letters."

I laughed, assuming he was joking. He was a renowned social psychologist, and his father was trained under Maslow, after all, but he didn't laugh back. Instead, he leaned in and said, "The system isn't built for your kind of curiosity."

That sentence landed in my body like a truth I didn't want to hear. He wasn't saying I wasn't capable. He was saying the system wasn't worthy of the kind of energy I wanted to give. That it might take more than it could offer in return, or that maybe the pursuit of titles and prestige wasn't the same thing as the pursuit of purpose.

At the time, I didn't know that millions of other people were having the same realization—questioning the institutions they once chased, wondering if the rules they'd been taught to follow were designed to keep them stuck.

The signs were already there; I was just too wrapped up in academia to notice them. The U.S. student loan crisis had reached record highs, with borrowers drowning in debt that often outweighed the value of their degrees. Across social media, entire communities were forming around the disillusionment of traditional career paths. People were rejecting hustle culture, quitting jobs that drained them, and openly discussing burnout, exploitation, and the myth of meritocracy.

Organizational psychologist and professor Dr. Anthony Klotz coined it The Great Resignation, but really, it was a reckoning. A mass awakening to the truth that chasing success as it's been defined—by productivity, prestige, and profit—often leads to disconnection, exhaustion, and despair. For the first time in decades, people weren't just leaving jobs. They were abandoning entire belief systems.

All of this occurred in early 2021 during the COVID-19 pandemic. The phenomenon was driven by various factors, including wage stagnation, limited opportunities for career advancement, hostile work environments, lack of benefits, inflexible remote-work policies, and long-standing job dissatisfaction, according to Klotz. The U.S. Bureau of Labor Statistics indicates that a record 4.5 million workers quit their jobs in March 2022, marking the peak of The Great Resignation. The industries most affected included accommodation and food services, retail, and healthcare. This mass exodus highlighted a growing discontent with traditional work structures and prompted discussions about the need for systemic changes in the workplace.

It wasn't laziness; it was resistance. Resistance to being told that their worth was defined by their output. Resistance to a capitalist model that prizes efficiency over humanity. To a system that only rewards the few at the expense of the many.

And with that resistance came imagination. People began creating new definitions of success—ones that prioritized rest, autonomy, creativity, and community. Workers in nontraditional industries began organizing and unionizing. Artists, therapists, and small business owners began carving out spaces that centered purpose over profit. Even those who remained within the system started asking bigger questions:

What am I working toward?

Who is benefiting from my burnout?

Is this the kind of life I want to sustain?

Around the same time, we began to see cultural shifts that signaled a collective desire to opt out of the hustle altogether. Our bread-baking habits during lockdown transitioned into a "soft life" aesthetic that exploded on social media—tradwife content, slow living, homesteading, even cottagecore—all trends revealing an undercurrent of tiredness of a society that equates worth with productivity. While some of these movements are problematic in their gender politics or racial undertones, their popularity revealed something important: People were tired of measuring success by burnout. They no longer wanted to strive for a life that looks good on paper but feels hollow in practice. These trends weren't just about aesthetics—they were subtle acts of resistance against a system that glorifies overwork and rewards only those who play by outdated rules. Our current systems are failing to meet our emotional, relational, and psychological needs, and people are finally *doing* something about it.

To truly heal, we have to redefine what success looks like—not by chasing outdated ideals of productivity and prestige, but by honoring alignment, well-being, and our inherent worth beyond what we can produce.

Dr. Abrams knew that. He never doubted my abilities. He just knew I craved impact, not title, and he was reflective—and critical—enough to acknowledge the system wasn't built to make that type of work possible.

We are not meant to be machines. And yet, we've been conditioned to measure our value by output and accolades and by how many hours of work we can cram into a day. But what happens when the system we're told to trust doesn't deliver on its promises? What happens when we work hard, follow the rules, and still come up short—not because we failed, but because the game was rigged?

This is where resistance becomes a form of wisdom.

To resist isn't to rebel blindly, but to see clearly. It's to name the ways the systems we've been taught to revere—academia, capitalism, the corporate ladder—have kept us striving instead of thriving. It's to choose, over and over again, to live in alignment with our values, even when it means disappointing the expectations that were handed to us.

You don't have to abandon ambition to redefine success. You just have to decide whose version of success you're striving for.

Maybe it doesn't look like a Ph.D. or a six-figure salary. Maybe it looks like flexible hours, nervous system regulation, or the ability to take a walk at noon. Maybe it's not your job title that defines you, but how you show up in the spaces that matter—your friendships, your family, your community, your art. Maybe fulfillment isn't found in your resume, but in the way you feel when you wake up in the morning.

Redefining success means giving yourself permission to opt out of the life you were told you should want and, instead, ask, "What kind of life *actually* feels good to live?"

Think of Sam, the corporate rebel I met in Patagonia who quit her job because she saw right through the system. She realized the ladder she was climbing wasn't actually leading her where she wanted to go, and instead of pushing harder, she paused. She pivoted. She quit her job and spent time backpacking South America before making her next career move. Sam chose to build a life that honored her values, not her resume.

That kind of clarity doesn't come easily. The systems we're taught to trust—the ones that promise safety, status, or success—often lead us down paths paved with burnout. We follow the rules. We do what we're "supposed to do." And somewhere along the way, many of us lose sight of who we are, what we want, and what matters most. We get degrees we're told we need. We accept jobs that drain us. We measure our worth in deadlines and deliverables. All the while, our nervous systems are screaming for something slower, softer, more sustainable.

Some people keep climbing. Others collapse. But more and more, people are choosing to rebel.

Not out of spite, but out of self-respect. The rebels are redefining what it means to be successful. They're choosing wholeness over hustle, and they're reminding the rest of us that fulfillment isn't found in chasing what you're told you "should" want—it's found in the honesty about what you actually *need*.

That's why Dr. Abrams's words landed the way they did. When he told me I didn't need a Ph.D. to do something meaningful, that I could meet all of my career goals without tying myself to academia, I felt something crack open. Until then, I hadn't questioned the path I was on. I believed, like so many of us do, that more credentials equated to more value. That prestige meant purpose. That if I wanted to be taken seriously, I needed to play the game.

But Dr. Abrams knew better. He had spent his entire adult life inside the very system I was trying to prove myself to, and instead of encouraging me to pursue more accolades, he told the truth: Academia is an archaic, political institution. One that was never designed for thinkers like me—or for anyone, really, who values innovation over tradition, connection over competition, or wisdom over elitism. It rewards conformity, not creativity. Hierarchy, not collaboration. And as much as academics talk about change, they often resist the very disruption that growth requires.

So I listened. I went on to graduate from New York University with a master's degree in mental health counseling, and then I carried on with my life—and my career. Now, I'm accomplishing everything I've ever dreamed of (and more). When I stopped chasing someone else's version of success, I started building something new—something honest and far more aligned with my purpose—and now I run one of New York City's largest affordable therapy practices. And I spearheaded a community-driven mental health campaign to raise ten thousand dollars to provide no-cost therapy to marginalized teens and young adults in Brooklyn. I say this not to brag, but to show you what is possible when you simply step outside the boxes that society tries to shove you in.

Walking away from the outdated system of academia was the most radical and freeing thing I could do, and I wasn't alone.

All around me, I started noticing others doing the same—walking away from jobs and corporations that once promised fulfillment and, instead, forging their own paths. Some left high-paying executive positions just to open small businesses. Others left academia, not because they couldn't "cut it," but because they realized their creativity and passion were stifled by bureaucracy and burnout. Many began freelancing, consulting, or creating online platforms to share their expertise on their own terms.

It wasn't a mass exodus without fear. It was a movement rooted in something deeper: the belief that we are allowed to question the systems we're born into. We are allowed to rewrite the rules. That's the thing about resistance—it doesn't always look like protest. Sometimes it looks like rest. Even quitting. Choosing a slower, quieter life that nobody applauds you for, but one that finally feels like it's *yours*.

We often associate resistance with confrontation, but more often, it shows up in small, radical choices: unsubscribing from hustle culture, turning down opportunities that feel misaligned, saying no to burnout and yes to boundaries, choosing depth over visibility, or presence over perfection. These decisions may not make headlines, but they signal a shift that's already reshaping our collective values.

And these shifts are not only personal; they're political. When millions of people begin questioning what they've been taught to value, the ripple effect extends far beyond the individual. It changes what we prioritize in leadership. It influences how we design workspaces, classrooms, and policies. It challenges entire industries to do better. Movements like The Nap Ministry, mutual aid networks, and unionization in previously unorganized sectors didn't emerge from nowhere. They popped up because people started paying attention—and asking better questions, just like Sam.

Questions like:

What kind of world are we sustaining when rest is framed as laziness?

What happens when mental health becomes a privilege instead of a right?

Who benefits from our burnout, and who profits from our silence?

These are not abstract questions. They are the foundation of systemic change. Because the truth is, we can't heal in systems that depend on our disconnection. We can't thrive in cultures that reward self-betrayal. And we cannot redefine success unless we're willing to examine who originally defined it, and *why*.

That's what this chapter is really about. Not just resisting broken systems, but remembering that we are allowed to build new ones. Systems that center purpose. Systems that respect rest. Systems that honor humanity, not just productivity. Redefining success isn't a rejection of ambition. It's a reclamation of meaning.

We've seen this spirit of resistance before. Back in 2011, the Occupy Wall Street movement erupted in Zuccotti Park, just a subway ride from where I now run my therapy practice. What started as a protest against economic inequality and corporate greed became a global call to dismantle the systems that consolidate power among the few while leaving the rest to fend for scraps. "We are the 99%" wasn't just a slogan—it was a refusal to keep pretending the system was fair. The movement's physical presence may have faded, but its legacy lives on in today's collective disillusionment and grassroots organizing.

In many ways, we're still occupying—just differently now. Instead of sleeping in tents on Wall Street, we're occupying conversations, boardrooms, classrooms, and social feeds with questions that refuse to go away:

Why do so many work full-time and still struggle to afford housing?

Why are students drowning in debt for degrees that lead nowhere?

Why do billionaires get tax breaks while teachers crowdsource basic supplies?

These aren't isolated issues; they're systemic patterns—and people are responding by organizing in ways we haven't seen in decades. Unions are gaining momentum in industries once considered unorganizable: baristas, warehouse workers, digital media staff, therapists, adjunct professors. These efforts are about far more than just wages and benefits. People are organizing to preserve their dignity. They're finally saying, "Enough," to the systems that demand their labor while eroding their humanity. They're reclaiming collective power in a culture that worships individualism.

The debate around higher education reflects this, too. For decades, a college degree was positioned as the great equalizer. A ticket to upward mobility. But now, more people are beginning to question, *Equalizer for whom? Who is actually served by these institutions?* The truth is, higher education was always exclusionary—historically reserved for the elite and designed to perpetuate class divides. Today, that exclusivity persists in new forms: in astronomical tuition rates, exploitative adjunct labor, bloated administrative hierarchies, and a curriculum that often prioritizes Eurocentric perspectives while claiming to be "universal."

And still, we tell people to take out loans they may never be able to repay. We frame education as a personal responsibility rather than a public good. We shame those who don't "make it" through the pipeline, while refusing to question the pipeline itself. We're taught that a degree equals success, but we aren't taught to wonder, *Success for whom?* and *At what cost?*

Critics will argue, "Well, you don't have to go to college. No one forced you to take out those loans." True, but that logic ignores the cultural conditioning and structural pressure baked into our society. From the time we're children, we're taught that college is the only respectable path forward—that without a degree, we'll be flipping burgers or stuck in a dead-end job for life, and that both of these paths are inherently "wrong." Even further, for many first-generation students, BIPOC students, or those raised in poverty, college isn't just a dream—it's framed as the only legitimate escape route. So when people say, "You chose this," what they really mean is, "You should have known better," as if anyone is taught to question the very system that every adult in their life insisted would save them.

It's a classic bait-and-switch. We dangle the promise of social mobility in front of young people, wrap it in narratives about hard work and personal responsibility, and then blame them when the reality doesn't match the pitch. And when students graduate into a labor market that undervalues their degree, saddled with debt and disillusionment, we call them entitled. But this isn't entitlement; it's systemic betrayal.

I also want to clarify that there is nothing inherently wrong with flipping burgers or working a dead-end job if (1) you can afford to live a comfortable life and (2) you are doing so by choice and not by force from oppressive systems. The issue isn't the work itself. It's the fact that our society devalues certain forms of labor while failing to provide livable wages and basic dignity to the people who do it. When we talk about redefining success, we're not saying everyone needs to chase prestige—we're saying people deserve autonomy. Everyone deserves to choose a life that feels good to them without being punished by systems that reward status over substance.

What if we let go of the idea that success has to be purchased through debt or proved through prestige? What might learning look like if it weren't tied to debt, hierarchy, or elitism, but to curiosity, collaboration, and care? What if education wasn't a gatekeeper of worth, but a gateway to collective possibility? Imagine classrooms rooted in community needs, not competition. Mentorship without ego. Learning not as a part of the rat race, but as a lifelong relationship—with yourself, with others, and with the world around you.

Reimagining the Systems

Imagine if our public education system wasn't built on standardized testing and property taxes, but on shared values of equity, access, and emotional development. What if school funding wasn't determined by zip code, but by the collective understanding that every child—regardless of their neighborhood—deserves art, music, mental health support, and safe classrooms? What if teachers were paid like the architects of society they are, and students were taught not just to perform, but to question, connect, and co-create?

We'd see a generation of children who feel valued, not measured. Achievement gaps would narrow—not because students work harder, but because the system finally works for *them*. And instead of reproducing inequality, our schools could become the first real blueprint for collective care.

Finland and Canada stand as two of the most compelling examples of how equitable public education can shape a thriving society. In Finland, schools are publicly funded, teachers are highly trained and respected, and standardized testing is rare—yet students rank among the world's best while facing less pressure and receiving more emotional support (AQI, 2024). Canada's inclusive policies and equitable funding have led to high literacy, strong academic performance, and broad social mobility. Both show that when education centers equity and care over profit and competition, entire societies thrive.

Now imagine healthcare that isn't profit-driven, but community-rooted. What if care wasn't rationed by insurance status, but freely offered as a birthright? Imagine hospitals and clinics as spaces of healing, not billing—where doctors are trained to listen, mental health is treated with the same urgency as physical health, and wellness is measured not just in survival, but in quality of life. Where doulas and social workers are funded, not cut. Where no one has to choose between medication and groceries. We'd see fewer emergency room visits, more preventative care, and communities that are not just surviving, but thriving.

And taxes—what if taxes weren't just seen as a necessary evil, but as an act of collective care? Imagine a system where paying taxes felt like planting seeds, not watching your hard-earned money vanish. If transparency and trust replaced bureaucracy and suspicion, we could trace every dollar to the public libraries, food programs, and public transportation.

This isn't naive optimism or fantasy. These are real possibilities, ones we begin to shape every time we challenge the systems that tell us to compete instead of care. We've seen glimpses of what's possible through mutual aid networks, soup kitchens, community gardens, radical rest collectives, and public defenders who fight like hell for the people they serve. These are the blueprints. All we have to do is follow their lead and dare to dream bigger.

Cancel the American Dream

The American dream might be a lie, but maybe that's not the tragedy. Maybe the real tragedy is how long we believed it, or how many years we spent trying to fit ourselves into systems that were never designed with our wholeness in mind. How many parts of ourselves we silenced—our creativity, our intuition, our rest—in service of a definition of success that was never ours to begin with.

But now we know better, and we're doing absolutely nothing about it.

Resistance, in all its forms, is not failure. It's wisdom. And redefining success isn't an escape from responsibility—it's a return to alignment. We can still dream big. We can still build. But we get to ask better questions about what we're building and who it's for.

And maybe, just maybe, the most radical success isn't in rising to the top of broken systems—but in daring to imagine something new.

The Success Audit

We inherit ideas of success long before we can question them. They come from our families, schools, workplaces, and the culture at large, shaping how we measure our worth without ever asking if those measures belong to *us*. The Success Audit is a way to pause, zoom out, and separate what you've been taught from what you actually believe.

Grab a piece of paper and draw a line down the middle. On the left, write "Inherited Success" and list the definitions, milestones, and expectations you've absorbed from others. On the right, write "My Success," and name what *actually* feels meaningful to you—what makes you feel alive, grounded, and aligned. Be honest. You may find that some of your inherited definitions still matter, but many no longer fit. The goal isn't to reject everything you've been taught; it's to choose with intention.

Here's mine:

Inherited Success	My Success
Work hard and save money	Stop hustling for every dollar
Pursue higher education	Prioritize expanding your business
Titles and awards are power	Generate passive income
Middle class is respectable	Burnout is not success
Upper class is greedy	Balance work and play
Don't spend frivolously	Don't pause life just to save
Live a simple life	Invest your savings
Saving > spending	Build generational wealth
You do what you have to do	Don't fear wealth
Put your head down and grind	If you're not present, you're failing
Retire by 65	Retire early and *live*

When you look at your lists side-by-side, notice where they align and where they diverge. Those divergences are your invitations. Opportunities to stop striving toward someone else's life and start building your own.

In my own Success Audit, my "Inherited Success" list read like the blueprint of my working-class, immigrant ancestors—keep your head down, work hard, don't spend too much, and whatever you do, don't take risks that could jeopardize stability. On the other side, my own success list read more like a visionary—expand, invest, create ease, trust that abundance is possible, and prioritize presence over production. The tension between these two mindsets is physiological. My nervous system was wired for decades to equate safety with scarcity, to brace for loss before it came. Shifting into my own definition of success required me to retrain my body to feel safe in rest, tolerate the uncertainty of risk, and believe that expansion doesn't always mean *danger*.

Both are completely valid and honorable ways of being, but only one allows for a full-body exhale that is critical in breaking the cycle of intergenerational trauma. In the next chapter, we explore what happens when we begin to unlearn the systems we were taught to serve and, instead, choose to let go. To surrender the illusion of control, embrace uncertainty, and find freedom—not in what we hold onto, but in what we're finally willing to release.

8

The Fight for Feeling

A war is being waged on U.S. soil, and it's not on people, policies, or public trust—it's on empathy.

Polarized media. Dog-whistle politics. Performative outrage. Compassion fatigue. All of it chips away at our capacity to see each other clearly and to care deeply. We struggle to sit with discomfort long enough to create real change. This isn't just emotional erosion; it's strategic. If we stop caring, we stop fighting—and the systems built on apathy remain exactly as they are.

Take the Black Lives Matter movement. What began as a desperate, grieving cry for justice following the 2013 acquittal of Trayvon Martin's murderer, George Zimmerman, became one of the largest social movements in U.S. history. Millions took to the streets in 2020—not just in major cities, but in small towns across all fifty states—demanding structural change following multiple instances of police brutality. Demanding that Black lives be treated as equal. Demanding accountability, not just from individual police officers, but from the very systems that produce harm.

For a brief moment, it felt like something might shift. Corporations issued public statements. Police departments promised reform. Books on racial justice topped bestseller lists. People posted black squares, donated to bail funds, and promised to "do better."

And then?

The headlines faded. The black squares disappeared. Policy reforms stalled or were actively reversed. In many cities, including New York, funding for programs like the Crime Victim Assistance Program (CVAP), which supports survivors of violent crimes, was slashed by millions. Meanwhile, police budgets remained intact, and, in some cases, they grew.

The system flexed. It absorbed the outrage and then went back to business as usual because that's what systems designed to maintain power do: They perform empathy long enough to avoid disruption. They nod, they reposition, and then they stall. And when the public inevitably burns out, they tighten their grip.

If you look closely, the same cycle played out in the fight for LGBTQ+ rights. For decades, queer and trans communities were erased, criminalized, and scapegoated. Then, slowly, the communities were tokenized—appearing in ad campaigns, TV shows, and company Pride floats long before they had basic legal protections. Rainbow capitalism became the norm: brands slapping a rainbow on their logo each June, parading through Pride with vague slogans about inclusion while donating to politicians who actively pushed anti-LGBTQ+ legislation. It was empathy as optics, not action.

And policy? Policy has always lagged behind performance. It wasn't until 2015 that same-sex marriage became legal nationwide. Not because our systems evolved with compassion, but because enough pressure forced their hand. And even now, nearly a decade later, trans rights are under relentless attack. Hundreds of anti-LGBTQ+ bills, most targeting transgender youth, have been introduced in state legislatures across the country. Basic access to healthcare, gender-affirming care, and safe schools remains unstable, contingent on political whims. Even now, as I'm writing this, the Supreme Court is receiving pressure to overturn Obergefell, its landmark ruling legalizing same-sex marriage. This is 2025.

Meanwhile, corporations still profit from queer aesthetics and allyship language while remaining silent as those same communities are targeted by policy and hate. The message is clear: We'll perform care when it's convenient, but we will not protect you when it counts.

Take Florida's "Don't Say Gay" law—officially known as the Parental Rights in Education Act—as a case study. Signed into law in 2022, it prohibits classroom instruction on sexual orientation and gender identity in certain grade levels and was quickly expanded to apply through twelfth grade. The language is broad and vague, which created a chilling effect: Teachers are afraid to display safe space stickers, introduce books with LGBTQ+ characters, or even acknowledge the existence of queer families.

Supporters framed the law as a way to protect children and preserve "parental rights," but for LGBTQ+ students and educators, the impact has been one of erasure, fear, and shame. It wasn't about protecting anyone—it was about control. About dictating whose stories are allowed to be told and whose identities are deemed too "controversial" to name.

This is how systems push back against empathy. Just when there's a rise in visibility and connection, when real understanding begins to take hold, laws like this are passed to sever that progress. Discomfort, not safety, becomes the norm for marginalized groups. Performative care might appear in the form of pride campaigns or rainbow-themed packaging, but behind the curtain, the policies often say the opposite: "We do not see you. We will not protect you."

The mental health ramifications are profound. According to The Trevor Project's 2024 national survey, 39 percent of LGBTQ+ young people seriously considered attempting suicide, with rates increasing to 46 percent among transgender and nonbinary youth. Furthermore, 90 percent of LGBTQ+ youth reported that their well-being was negatively impacted due to recent politics. These statistics underscore the disconnect between the purported intent of such laws and their real-world effects. While framed as protective measures, policies like the "Don't Say Gay" law can exacerbate stigma, reduce access to supportive resources, and negatively affect the mental health of LGBTQ+ youth.

In a time marked by crisis after crisis, our collective ability to care—deeply, consistently, and courageously—is breaking down. Whether through political manipulation, media over-load, or sheer emotional exhaustion, we're witnessing not just a decline in empathy, but a deliberate dismantling of it.

From Outrage to Apathy

How do people keep caring when the crises never seem to stop? Realistically, they don't. There's a name for what we're experiencing: compassion fatigue. This happens when people are exposed to prolonged or repeated distress like natural disasters, mass shootings, human rights violations, political violence, and more, and their capacity to respond begins to erode. Not because they lack empathy, but because they've been overwhelmed by it. As the threats to our collective safety multiply, many people cope by numbing out. We aren't wired to metabolize this much pain.

Social media has only intensified this overload. One scroll can deliver a protest, a genocide, a school shooting, and a viral dance video, all in a matter of thirty seconds. Our brains aren't built to hold that contrast without consequence, so we dissociate. We compartmentalize. We double-tap and keep moving. And in doing so, we unknowingly train ourselves to witness suffering without feeling it.

Nowhere is this more evident than in the global response to the genocide in Gaza. For months, photos and videos of bombed-out buildings, injured children, and grieving families flooded our feeds, each image a cry for help. And yet, much of the world scrolls past, not because people don't care, but because they've been pushed beyond the limit of what they can hold. At a certain point, exposure stops eliciting empathy and starts reinforcing helplessness. People tell themselves, *This is just how the world is*. But that isn't acceptance; it's despair in disguise.

The tragedy is that our emotional disconnection doesn't come from apathy—it comes from overwhelm. And yet, systems benefit from this, too. If we're too tired to pay attention, we're too tired to fight. Our numbness becomes their insulation.

This tactic isn't new, but the second Trump administration mastered it. From the moment they took office, the public was hit with a relentless barrage of executive orders, controversial headlines, and inflammatory statements. The goal wasn't just policy change—it was desensitization. The sheer volume of chaos made it nearly impossible to keep up, let alone organize an effective response. One crisis blurred into the next.

Muslim travel bans, family separations at the border, roll-backs on environmental protections, deportations, attacks on press freedom—all stacked on top of each other until outrage became exhaustion. It was a strategy of emotional flooding: If people are overwhelmed, they stop reacting. If they stop reacting, the system can operate unchecked. The noise becomes the norm, and in the background, the damage quietly compounds.

It's important to note that not all stories are reported equally. Media coverage, especially in the U.S., is often filtered through lenses of race, nationality, and political interest. This shapes what we see, how much we see, and how we're expected to feel about it. In-group bias takes root, motivated reasoning kicks in, and empathy gaps grow.

Desensitized by Design

Motivated reasoning is the tendency to interpret new information in a way that aligns with our pre-existing beliefs. So even when people are presented with evidence of suffering—say, the mass displacement of Palestinians or rising temperatures caused by fossil fuel emissions—they may downplay it if it conflicts with their identity, ideology, or sense of control. The more emotionally charged the issue, the more people resist empathy, not because they're heartless, but because empathy threatens their worldview.

But empathy isn't just about worldview—it's also about regulation. When our nervous systems are dysregulated by fear, grief, or anger, we lose the capacity to connect. We become reactive, rigid, and defensive. That's why personal narratives are so powerful; they humanize complex issues. They regulate our nervous systems just enough to sit with discomfort rather than flee from it. They remind us that behind every statistic is a person, and behind every system is a story.

That reminder echoed in a 2022 PBS interview between journalist Jeffrey Brown and NYC Public Advocate Jumaane Williams, following the funeral of 12-year-old Kade Lewin—shot while sitting in a parked car.

"People are afraid. People are worried," Williams said. "And you understand why." He spoke candidly about the psychological toll that gun violence was taking on his community and the danger of letting fear go unchecked. "We have to have leadership that can address those fears, put them in context, so we don't get more afraid than we should be."

But instead of care and context, budget cuts were made. In that same year, New York City slashed over three million dollars from the CVAP, a critical resource for survivors of gun violence, domestic abuse, and trauma. The funding disappeared quietly, without outrage or headlines, because we were already exhausted. Already overwhelmed.

This is the paradox of public empathy: We respond urgently to acute, visible suffering—natural disasters, mass shootings, floods, fires—but struggle to sustain attention for long-term, systemic crises like climate change, white supremacy, or poverty. We donate to relief efforts, but not prevention. We show up for vigils, but not for policy. Our collective heart swells and then forgets. Not because we don't care, but because we've never been taught how to stay with the discomfort long enough to demand something better.

And yet, that's exactly what's required of us now.

We've been conditioned to compartmentalize pain. To rank certain tragedies as more "newsworthy" or "relatable" than others. A mass shooting barely breaks through the noise unless there's a uniquely horrifying detail like a toddler victim, a live-streamed video, or a glaring failure by law enforcement.

In the aftermath of the Robb Elementary School shooting in Uvalde, Texas, the public's attention was drawn not only to the tragic loss of nineteen children and two teachers but also to the law enforcement's delayed response. Despite officers arriving at the scene within minutes, it took 77 minutes before they confronted and neutralized the shooter. This delay became a focal point in media coverage, highlighting a broader societal pattern: the tendency to engage deeply with tragedies only when specific, often sensational, details emerge. In the case of Uvalde, the prolonged inaction by law enforcement became that focal point, prompting widespread outrage and discussions about police protocols and accountability—not about the rising number of mass shootings.

Such selective engagement reflects a phenomenon where the public's capacity for empathy and sustained attention is influenced by the uniqueness or shock value of certain aspects of a tragedy. This pattern underscores the challenges in maintaining consistent public discourse and action on systemic issues, especially when media narratives shift focus rapidly, and collective attention wanes. Understanding this dynamic is critical in addressing how society processes and responds to recurring tragedies, ensuring that the emphasis remains on comprehensive solutions rather than transient reactions to isolated details.

When I share that I've survived an abusive relationship, the questions I'm asked are almost always about the relationship itself:

Was it physical?

How long were you together?

How did you leave?

Rarely am I asked about the aftermath—about the slow, messy, and ongoing process of rebuilding trust with myself and others. No one asks:

How has that relationship shaped your experiences dating now?

What feels safe, and what doesn't?

What have you learned about love since?

These are the questions that lead to understanding, not just of what happened, but of how a person has lived and healed since. Without them, we risk reducing someone's entire story to their worst chapter instead of honoring the whole arc of their recovery. We get lost in the details and ignore the bigger picture.

That's why I created my relational trauma group—to shift the conversation from *what happened to you* to *how you've been shaped since.* The group is a space where survivors can explore the ripple effects of a trauma in a way that honors their resilience as much as their pain. We focus on the questions that often go unasked: What triggers your nervous system now, and why? Where have you found safety, and where does fear still linger? How have your beliefs about love, trust, and intimacy evolved?

Restoring Empathy at Scale

If apathy is learned, empathy can be relearned. We're not born indifferent. Indifference is a survival response to overwhelm, a habit shaped by systems that teach us to numb, ignore, and move on. But just as systems can erode empathy, they can also be rebuilt to cultivate it.

Restoring empathy at scale doesn't begin with more information—it begins with different infrastructures. We need public institutions that are not only functional but emotionally intelligent. Schools that teach emotional literacy alongside academic skills. Healthcare systems that treat trauma as a root cause, not a side effect. Media that prioritizes nuance and humanity over virality and outrage.

I think about the women in my relational trauma group—how they show up every week carrying invisible grief, shame, and years of feeling like their pain didn't matter. And I watch how slowly, over time, that begins to change. Not because someone gave them a solution, but because someone listened without flinching. Because someone made space for their story as it is without needing to minimize it or make it more palatable, like the rest of society. That, too, is systemic change. It's the result of containers that honor complexity and restore dignity. It's slow, it's intimate, and it matters.

We need collective rituals that help us metabolize grief, process harm, and reconnect with our shared humanity. In Rwanda, gacaca courts helped communities process the trauma of genocide through public dialogue and communal justice. In post-apartheid South Africa, the Truth and Reconciliation Commission used storytelling as a vehicle for collective healing. These are imperfect systems, but they show us what's possible when empathy is embedded into public life—not as a sentiment, but as a strategy.

On a local level, this might look like funding trauma-informed community centers, increasing access to mental health care, or training public servants in emotional regulation and conflict resolution. On a national scale, it could mean rewriting policies to center care over punishment and dialogue over division. Perhaps most importantly, it means resisting the urge to tune out. The more we build our personal capacity to stay present with suffering—not all of it, but some of it, intentionally and consistently—the more likely we are to become agents of systemic change. Empathy, after all, is not just a feeling. It's a muscle. It gets stronger the more we use it, and it weakens every time we look away.

So the question isn't just, "Why don't we care anymore?" It's "How will we choose to care now that we know we should?"

From Overwhelm to Action

Empathy is not infinite, but it is renewable. It fades when we're overwhelmed, but it can be restored through nervous system regulation, storytelling, and community care. We've been taught to protect ourselves from emotional pain by disconnecting, but that disconnection—when it becomes habitual—only ensures that systems of harm remain intact. Performative empathy might feel good in the moment, but without structural change, it's just another layer of insulation for the status quo.

Disconnection is not always apathy. Often, it's survival, but that doesn't mean we should accept numbness as the norm. We can learn to notice when we're withdrawing and ask ourselves why. We can rebuild our tolerance for discomfort, not by flooding ourselves with more tragedy, but by seeking out personal narratives and staying regulated enough to remain present. That's where empathy grows: not in viral outrage, but in quiet, sustained presence. Behind every statistic is a human being. Behind every system is a collection of decisions and the people who made them.

Next time you feel yourself pulling away from the news, avoiding a difficult conversation, or scrolling past a tragedy online, pause and try this three-part reset:

1. **Name what's happening in your body.**

   Don't force yourself to care—just notice your physiological state. Are your shoulders tense? Is your breath shallow? Is your heart rate elevated or, conversely, do you feel flat and heavy? These sensations are signals from your nervous system that you're overwhelmed or shutting down.

2. **Choose one human story.**

   Rather than trying to hold the weight of an entire crisis, focus on one person's story. Read a firsthand account. Watch an interview. Look at a photograph and imagine their daily life—their routines, their family, what they might be worrying about or hoping for. This prepares your nervous system from a place of connection, which is more sustainable than consuming endless headlines from a place of apathy.

3. **Take one small action.**

   Empathy is sustainable when it's paired with agency.

That action might be donating a small amount, signing a petition, attending a local event, having a conversation to raise awareness, or committing to following the story. You're not solving the crisis single-handedly. You're just reminding yourself that care still has a place in your life.

With practice, your nervous system begins to trust that staying present with discomfort won't break you, and that small, consistent actions can lead to meaningful change. Over time, this builds your capacity to feel deeply without shutting down, giving you a sustainable alternative to numbing out.

If we want to restore empathy on a systemic level, we have to stop outsourcing care to press releases and empty statements. We need emotional infrastructure—trauma-informed policies, social-emotional education, mental health support embedded in our schools and workplaces. We need systems that don't just rely on our empathy, but actively protect and nourish it. Because when people feel safe and seen, they care more. And when people care more, they act.

That's how we begin to fight back against the war on empathy—and in many ways, we've been losing. We're not incapable of care; we just haven't been given the tools to sustain it. The truth is, if we want a future where compassion isn't seen as naive, but necessary, we have to learn how to feel deeply and act wisely. We have to make space for discomfort. For nuance. For grief. Because the moment we stop feeling, we stop changing, and that's exactly what the systems that rely on our numbness are banking on.

Which brings us to the next chapter. If this chapter explored empathy at the macro, the next explores it at the micro: the individual. The systems may be massive, but every system is built and maintained by people. By individuals. And when one person decides to act with care, clarity, and courage, it can create ripple effects we never imagined. In the next chapter, we'll explore the science of prosocial behavior, the psychology of influence, and the radical idea that one person—when grounded in empathy—can be a powerful catalyst for collective change.

9

Harness the Power of One

We talk a lot about "changing the world" but forget that the world is just made up of people—each one capable of changing someone else's. Change often begins with a moment, not a movement.

Empathy doesn't require millions of followers. It doesn't need a trending hashtag or a viral speech. It needs a pause. A choice. A willingness to ask a hard question or sit beside someone in their pain. These small decisions, the ones we make in classrooms, offices, group chats, and grocery store lines, are the tipping points. They're neither dramatic nor glamorous, but they're powerful.

You don't need a platform to make an impact. You need presence, intention, and just enough courage to reach across whatever distance has been drawn between you and someone else. The people we've met so far—Jack, Maren, Matteo, River and Lucy, Brandon, Sam, Dr. Abrams, and the women in my relational trauma group—didn't set out to change the world, but they changed mine. And in doing so, they inspired me to write this book, which will ripple outwards to (ideally) millions of people, maybe changing them, too. These people are proof that transformation doesn't come from sweeping declarations, but from the accumulation of small, intentional acts.

Sam questioned a system she was told to trust, and in doing so, gave others permission to question, too.

Dr. Abrams offered one sentence that rerouted my path entirely.

Jack offered a moment of quiet, unconditional care, one that reminded me how powerful it can be to simply show up for someone, no strings attached.

The group members who sat in their pain together, week after week, learned to hold space for each other in ways that most institutions never will.

Each of them represents a thread in my story. On their own, they might seem small, but woven together, they create a tapestry of connection, courage, and care. A living example of what it looks like to resist disconnection and choose empathy. That's the heart of this chapter: the reminder that you are one of those threads, too.

Meaningful change doesn't always begin with institutions or movements, but with individuals—ordinary people making conscious choices to show up with empathy, disrupt indifference, and extend care.

We tend to underestimate the power of small moments. We wait for the sweeping change, the policy shift, the viral campaign—forgetting that those movements were often sparked by someone doing something quietly brave. Someone asking a better question or saying, "This isn't right," even if their voice shook. Someone choosing presence over passivity.

Sam didn't organize a protest or write a viral op-ed; she simply told the truth about how a system she once trusted had failed her. In doing so, she modeled a form of personal activism that doesn't look like rebellion, but is. She made it safer for others to speak up, to ask for more, and to redefine what success should actually feel like.

Dr. Abrams didn't overhaul the system. He offered a single sentence that gave me permission to step off a path I thought I was supposed to follow. It wasn't a grand gesture, but it was a lifeline of sorts. Sometimes that's all it takes: one person telling you that you don't need to prove your worth to a system that never saw your value to begin with.

Jack didn't call it activism when he showed up to help someone he barely knew. He didn't do it for credit or recognition. He did it because it was human. Because care, when offered without condition, has a way of reverberating outward. His one act of kindness rippled through the lives of others, creating a chain reaction of empathy that I still carry with me today.

And then there were the women in my relational trauma group—who showed up every week to sit in discomfort, to name the patterns that had shaped them, to witness and be witnessed. That space was sacred not because it was official or public or performative, but because it was consistent. The simple, repeated act of holding space for one another became an act of collective healing.

These are not isolated stories. They are a reflection of what is possible when people act with intention. When we stop asking, "Will this change the world?" and start asking, "Can this change one person's world?" because often, that's how it starts. One conversation, one act of care, one refusal to look away.

So here's my invitation to you: Recognize that your capacity for impact is not measured in followers, funding, or fanfare, but in your willingness to act when it would be easier to stay silent. Show up with empathy, even when it's inconvenient. Be the one who starts the ripple.

The Butterfly Effect

The idea that small actions can create large and lasting change isn't just poetic; it's science. The Butterfly Effect originated in the field of chaos theory, a branch of mathematics that studies how tiny changes in initial conditions can lead to vastly different outcomes over time. The term was popularized by meteorologist Edward Lorenz, who discovered in the 1960s that minor differences in weather modeling data could produce wildly divergent forecasts. In a 1972 talk titled "Predictability: Does the Flap of a Butterfly's Wings in Brazil Set Off a Tornado in Texas?", Lorenz suggested that even the smallest influence—like the flap of a butterfly's wings—could alter the course of complex systems (Lorenz, 1972).

While the concept originated in meteorology, it's since been adopted as a metaphor across disciplines from economics to philosophy and psychology. In the context of this book, the Butterfly Effect reminds us that the impact of empathy often unfolds in ways we can't predict or immediately see: a quiet act of care, a choice to listen instead of judge, a moment of vulnerability. These are not insignificant. In systems as complex as human relationships and society, even a single shift in behavior or belief can create ripple effects that extend far beyond our awareness.

That's the hope embedded in every story shared in this book. That a single moment—like Jack offering care, Sam questioning authority, or you deciding to reconnect instead of retreat—can move the needle. Not dramatically and not all at once, but meaningfully. And over time, that meaning builds. It spreads. It invites others to act with a little more courage and a little more compassion. That's how change happens—not just on stages or in government systems, but in coffee shops, classrooms, text messages, and therapy rooms. In a world that often demands we do something big to matter, the Butterfly Effect, regardless of whether it is real or not, is a powerful reminder that we can start small—and that just might be the most powerful place to begin.

How to Practice Empathy Every Day

The good news is you don't need to be a policymaker, influencer, or activist to change the world. You just need to start where you are—with the people you interact with, the systems you participate in, and the choices you make every day. Here are some practical strategies to help you harness the power of one:

1. Interrupt Disconnection in Real Time

When someone shares something painful, resist the urge to fix, debate, or distract. Instead, offer presence. Try saying, "That sounds really hard. Do you want to talk more about it, or would you rather sit together in silence?" Simply being with someone, rather than attempting to solve their pain, is one of the most profound forms of care.

2. Assume Complexity, Not Simplicity

Instead of flattening people into headlines or assumptions, pause and remind yourself, *I don't know their full story*. Whether it's someone who cut you off in traffic or a neighbor with different political beliefs, remembering complexity allows empathy to take root where judgment might otherwise grow.

3. Practice Micro-Repair

Small moments of conflict or disconnection don't have to escalate. Whether it's a short apology, a clarifying follow-up, or a thoughtful text, micro-repairs help build trust and resilience in your relationships. They show that you value connection more than being right.

4. Tell Your Stories—and Invite Theirs

Sharing vulnerably (when safe to do so) invites others into deeper relationships. You don't have to share your deepest pain; sometimes, simply saying, "That reminds me of something I've felt, too" opens space for connection. And when someone shares with you, listen with the intention to understand, not respond.

5. Engage Locally, Not Just Virtually

Online awareness is important, but in-person action creates embodied empathy. Volunteer. Show up to community forums. Support a mutual aid network.

Ask your local schools, shelters, or hospitals what they need. Grounding your values in physical action makes them tangible.

6. **Revisit Your Circles of Influence**

Think about the spaces where your voice carries weight—your workplace, your family, your classroom, your group chat. What would it look like to name something unjust, advocate for someone unheard, or start a new norm? Big movements start with conversations in small rooms.

7. **Practice Proximity**

Intentionally move towards experiences you don't understand. Spend time in communities that are different from your own, attend public forums, volunteer, or even follow storytellers from other cultures online. Proximity builds empathy through lived context—not assumption. Bryan Stevenson, a widely acclaimed public interest lawyer who helped release over 135 wrongfully accused prisoners on death row, said, "You cannot understand someone from a distance. Move closer."

8. Take Care of Your Nervous System

Empathy doesn't flourish in a state of burnout. Rest, regulate, and recharge. That may mean stepping away from the news, seeking therapy, or simply going for a walk. Empathy is a resource—and like any resource, it needs replenishment.

The Cost of Turning Away

Choosing empathy doesn't always feel easy, but choosing disconnection has a cost, too. When we repeatedly look away from suffering—ours or someone else's—we don't just protect ourselves from discomfort, we risk losing something much greater: our humanity.

History is full of people who turned away for too long. People who ignored suffering until it no longer registered as wrong. People who suppressed their own pain so deeply that numbness became second nature, and cruelty followed close behind.

Take Adolf Eichmann, one of the architects of the Holocaust. In Hannah Arendt's groundbreaking work, *Eichmann in Jerusalem* (1963), she coined the term "the banality of evil" to describe how ordinary people commit horrific acts when they stop questioning, stop feeling, and start obeying. Eichmann didn't appear monstrous—he was disturbingly average. It was his lack of reflection, his failure to empathize, that made his actions so dangerous. He, like many during the Holocaust, turned away from the humanity of others and, in doing so, lost his own.

For my true crime junkies, consider Ted Bundy, whose charm and charisma masked a chilling emotional detachment. In psychological interviews, Bundy displayed a total lack of empathy and remorse, often describing his crimes in detached, clinical language. Forensic psychologists have long noted that while not all people who lack empathy become violent, nearly all serial killers show signs of severe empathy deficits early on—usually stemming from trauma, emotional neglect, or chronic disconnection in childhood (Hare, 1999).

Even in the political sphere, we've seen how desensitization to suffering creates space for authoritarianism. Leaders who routinely dehumanize others—immigrants, the poor, political opponents—rely on public apathy to maintain power. The erosion of empathy is strategic. If you stop caring, you stop resisting. Fortunately, the opposite is also true.

Empathy is how people have ended genocides, toppled authoritarian regimes, and rewritten laws. It's how survivors of apartheid, internment camps, and family separation have found the strength to tell their stories, forcing the world to pay attention. Turning toward pain is not just an act of care; it's an act of courage. And sometimes, it's an act of revolution.

Responding to What's Right in Front of You

Turning toward doesn't always mean confronting evil or dismantling corrupt systems, especially not overnight. Sometimes it's recognizing the power and privilege we do have, then choosing to use it. For me, that moment came when I launched a free therapy initiative through my group therapy practice, Well Psychotherapy. I was overwhelmed by the sheer number of inquiries—especially from young adults—who couldn't access affordable mental health care. It felt unjust, and constantly turning them away left a sour taste in my mouth. And while I know I can't fix the entire system, I knew I could respond to the need in front of me—so I did.

I shared the stories. I asked for help. And together, with friends, clients, colleagues, and complete strangers, we raised ten thousand dollars to fund free therapy sessions for those who needed them most. It wasn't a viral campaign or a national movement; it was a collective act of care. A moment of saying, "We see you. You matter." That's the thing about turning toward pain or injustice: It's rarely grand or dramatic. It's often quiet, rooted in ordinary people making intentional choices to show up anyway.

Our one-night art auction fundraiser showcased local artists, all of them carrying historically marginalized identities, who donated their work for the greater good of our shared community. They witnessed a need that felt greater than their own and decided to show up. Those who attended, most of whom had zero connection to the artists or Well Psychotherapy, showed up, too. They purchased a ticket knowing 100 percent of proceeds went directly to the campaign, and some even opened their wallets and left with new art—art that carries meaning far greater than something they might have ordered online.

Learning to Let People In

Empathy wasn't always my default. Quite the opposite, actually. I've had seasons where I felt guarded, self-protective, and deeply disconnected—not just from others, but from myself. Pain has a way of doing that. Certain experiences—like pulling a friend over the wall of my hometown bridge and later visiting him in an inpatient psychiatric unit, or cutting off contact with my parents when the exchange between us caused more harm than good—shattered me so profoundly that it felt safer to retreat into myself than to risk being hurt again. I stopped offering softness because I didn't know where it would land.

When your trust has been broken in ways that shake your core, it's hard to believe that connection can be safe. I learned to keep people at arm's length. I filtered every relationship through the lens of hypervigilance, and I wore my independence like armor, convinced I didn't need anyone but myself. Somewhere along the way, that started to change. A lot of it started with my best friend, Jules.

Jules didn't fix me. She didn't rush in with answers or platitudes. What she did was infinitely more powerful—she stayed. She witnessed. She cared with consistency and without conditions. Slowly, her presence chipped away at the wall I had built around my heart. Not by demanding vulnerability, but by modeling what safety could look like.

One year, we were out celebrating Jules's birthday when someone asked her, casually, who her best friend was. Without skipping a beat, she said, "Laura." I turned my head, caught off guard. It felt like no one had ever said that about me before—at least not in *that* way. For a second, I felt my body tense, bracing for the disbelief or dismissal I used to carry like instinct, but it never came. Instead, I watched her continue the conversation, completely at ease, as if her answer was obvious. And in that moment, something softened. I settled into the quiet safety of being chosen—being seen not for what I could offer, but for who I was. It was the kind of friendship I had always wanted but wasn't sure would ever find me. One rooted in presence, history, and the kind of care that doesn't flinch when things get hard.

If you've ever felt this way–guarded, alone, or like real connection is just out of reach—I want you to know you're not broken. You're protecting something precious. You've learned, maybe through pain or disappointment, that it hasn't always been safe to let people in. That kind of wisdom is hard-earned. And still, I want to remind you: You're allowed to want more.

You deserve to be chosen without having to prove your worth. You deserve steady love, the kind that doesn't disappear when things get heavy. You deserve to feel safe in someone's presence, to relax your shoulders, to laugh without scanning the room for judgment. You deserve relationships that remind you it's OK to exhale.

Healing doesn't require you to open yourself all at once. Sometimes it starts with one person, one moment, one, "I'm here." Let that be enough for now. Letting someone in, even if it's just one person, shifts how we relate to the world. Once I felt what it was like to be held in the kind of friendship where I didn't have to earn love or prove my value, something in me softened. I stopped seeing everyone as a potential threat or disappointment. I started seeing people as complex, hurting, and trying, just like me.

It's easier to extend empathy when you've experienced it firsthand. When you know what it feels like to be truly seen, it becomes harder to look away from someone else's pain. When someone's consistent presence shows you that connection can be safe, you begin to trust your own capacity to offer that safety to others.

Letting people in teaches us that we're not alone in our tenderness. And when we stop bracing for harm, we open ourselves up to deeper understanding, more honest communication, and real relational repair. That's when empathy becomes more than an ideal—it becomes a reflex. A way of moving through the world with less armor and more intention.

If you're reading this, you're already doing the work. You're reflecting, you're questioning, and you're choosing not to look away—and that matters. It matters more than you know. The world doesn't change all at once; it changes when one person decides to show up with more care. When one person pauses before judging, or takes the risk to let someone in.

If you've ever felt like your voice doesn't carry, your effort doesn't matter, or your story is too small to make a difference, remember this:

Your presence can be the turning point in someone's day.

Your care can create space for someone else to heal.

Your courage to connect might be the very thing that inspires someone else to do the same.

We don't always get to see the ripple effect of our actions, but that doesn't mean they aren't there. In fact, the most powerful change often happens quietly—in ordinary moments, between ordinary people, who decide to act with intention. You don't need to be a leader, a healer, or a hero. You just need to be human, willing, and open. That is the power of one.

10

Put Empathy into Action

I n a world brimming with division, despair, and disen-
gagement, what gives me hope isn't sweeping policies or
headline-making movements—it's the glimmers. The quiet,
human-scale acts that remind us we still belong to one another.

Again, my mind turns to March 2020, when the world
came to a halt and fear settled into every corner of our lives.
In cities like Milan, New York, and Madrid, apartment lights
flickered on as dusk fell—but instead of sinking into silence,
something incredible happened. People stepped out onto their
balconies and began to sing. A grandmother crooned lullabies
into the night air. A violinist played "Ave Maria" while neighbors lit candles from their windows. In one building, a teenager
with a speaker and a mic began hosting nightly concerts, taking
requests shouted across courtyards. It wasn't just entertainment, it was a balm. A lifeline. A way of saying, "I'm still here.

You're not alone." And somehow, despite everything, it made us feel a little less afraid.

I think about the summer of 2020, shortly after lockdown restrictions were lifted, when people across the country flooded the streets following the murder of George Floyd. It wasn't just the marches in major cities that moved me—it was the collective uprising across towns where protest had never been part of the culture. Rural highways lined with hand-painted signs. High school students organizing teach-ins. Grandmothers handing out water bottles to strangers. In my own neighborhood, just one block south of the epicenter of the Manhattan protests in Washington Square Park, I remember walking behind a group of children holding cardboard signs. Their voices were small, but mighty. Their parents, marching beside them, demanding justice and teaching their children what it looks like to show up. To care. It felt like a collective exhale of grief, reckoning, and solidarity. For a moment, we remembered what it meant to rise together.

I think about the aftermath of hurricanes, wildfires, and floods. The way neighbors become first responders. Strangers wading through water just to rescue each other. Volunteers collecting diapers, flashlights, and food in church basements. People opening their homes, donating their time, and asking, "What do you need?" not because they have to, but because they *can*.

In January 2025, Los Angeles endured a catastrophic wildfire season—over 57,000 acres scorched, more than 18,000 structures destroyed, and at least thirty lives lost. Amid the devastation, something remarkable happened: Spontaneous volunteer convoys rushed into evacuation zones, rescuing people, their pets, and livestock, despite their own homes being at risk. Local and national funds poured in—city relief grants offered direct aid, while concert audiences at "FireAid" raised millions for immediate and future rebuilding measures. These responses didn't fix everything, but they showed that amid climate catastrophe and systemic inertia, our impulse to care remains alive.

Even amid the rise of dog-whistle politics and deepening social divides, I've seen people pause. Reflect. Change. I've sat in rooms where someone admitted they used to hold a belief rooted in fear or ignorance—and then, after listening to another person's story, they chose to do better. One conversation. One open heart. That's all it takes sometimes to begin a shift.

These moments don't always make headlines, but they leave an imprint. They remind us that empathy is still alive, still reachable, still possible—even in a world that tells us otherwise. Because when systems fail us, people still show up. We sing. We march. We feed each other. We remember that we belong to something larger than ourselves. And in those moments, however fleeting, we don't just survive—we come alive again. Empathy is not a passive feeling; it's an active choice we make in the face of adversity, division, and disillusionment. This chapter explores how putting empathy into action, even through the smallest of gestures, can rebuild faith in humanity, foster collective resilience, and create a future defined not by fear, but by connection.

The Science of Social Connection

If empathy is the emotional spark, connection is the fuel that keeps the fire burning. This is biological. Human beings are wired to bond, to belong, and to care for one another in ways that have been fundamental to our survival as a species. From the earliest tribal communities to modern suburbia, our nervous systems have evolved to co-regulate, synchronize, and attune to each other. Connection isn't just a nice-to-have—it's essential.

At the core of this is our brain's mirror neuron system, which we have learned activates not only when we perform an action, but when we observe someone else performing it. When you see someone cry, wince in pain, or erupt into laughter, your brain lights up as if it were happening to you. That's not just emotional resonance—it's empathy in action. Our brains are built to feel with others.

And it's not just our brains. The polyvagal theory, pioneered by Dr. Stephen Porges, shows us that our bodies constantly scan for cues of safety or danger in social environments. When we feel connected—through eye contact, touch, a gentle tone—our parasympathetic nervous system, the one responsible for our most relaxed state, kicks in, calming us and allowing us to rest, digest, and relate. This is what Porges (2004) calls "neuroception of safety," and it's foundational to emotional regulation and co-regulation. In short: Safety makes connection possible, and connection helps us stay safe.

Empathy also activates the brain's default mode network—a system responsible for self-reflection and understanding others' perspectives. When this network is healthy and engaged, we're more likely to interpret people's behavior with curiosity rather than judgment. We imagine their inner world. We see context instead of caricature.

Even at a group level, the science is striking. Researchers studying collective effervescence—a term coined by sociologist Émile Durkheim (1912)—have found that when people gather for shared emotional experiences, like concerts, protests, religious rituals, or even sports games, they often report a sense of transcendence, unity, and purpose (Gabriel, Valenti & Young, 2017). These moments of shared emotion don't just feel good; they remind us of our interdependence. They make empathy more accessible because they remove the illusion of separateness.

And yet, in modern society, we've never been more distracted, over-scheduled, or siloed. We swipe past people instead of looking at them. We scroll through suffering instead of sitting with it. But the science is clear: Connection heals, not just individually, but collectively. It makes us braver. It improves mental health outcomes. It builds trust. It reduces polarization. And it sets the stage for large-scale change.

The question isn't whether we're wired for empathy—it's whether we're willing to fight for the conditions that allow it to thrive.

Where We're Headed If We Don't Reconnect

Disconnection is becoming more than just personal—it's a societal trajectory. When empathy fades from our collective fabric, we're left with isolation, polarization, and a slow erosion of the social trust that binds us. We see it already: rising loneliness, rampant misinformation, growing hostility between communities and identities. The more we turn inward or against each other, the harder it becomes to find our way back. If we don't make a conscious effort to return to each other, to reconnect, we risk creating a world where fear outweighs compassion, division becomes the norm, and humanity feels more like a burden than a gift.

We're already witnessing the early symptoms of a society in retreat from itself. In the U.S., rates of loneliness have reached epidemic proportions. A 2023 Gallup poll found that one in four Americans reported feeling lonely "most of the time," with young adults and older populations most acutely affected (Gallup, 2023). Loneliness isn't just emotionally painful—it's physically dangerous. Research from the U.S. Surgeon General's 2023 advisory compares the health risks of chronic loneliness to smoking fifteen cigarettes a day, linking it to increased risks of cardiovascular disease, dementia, and premature death (U.S. Department of Health and Human Services, 2023).

At the same time, polarization is deepening, not just politically, but socially and relationally. People are more likely than ever to live, work, and socialize within ideological silos. Pew Research (2022) data shows that nearly 60 percent of Americans feel they have few or no friends with differing political beliefs, and many report avoiding conversations with family members to sidestep conflict. This level of fragmentation undermines trust—not just in institutions, but in each other.

Misinformation thrives in disconnected societies. When we lose our ability to empathize with people outside our own worldview, it becomes easier to dehumanize them. Online platforms, fueled by algorithms that reward outrage and extremity, amplify this effect, creating echo chambers where fear and bias are reinforced rather than questioned. Hate crimes in the U.S. have risen for four consecutive years (FBI, 2024), and extremist violence—both domestic and global—is often rooted not only in ideology, but in alienation.

When we turn away from empathy, we don't just become indifferent; we become vulnerable to movements that offer the illusion of connection through belonging to an "us" defined against a "them." This is how nationalism grows. How conspiracy theories spread. How authoritarianism gains traction in democratic spaces. And it's not hypothetical—it's already happening.

Politicians know this. They know that fear, isolation, and disconnection breed susceptibility, and they exploit it. In the early days of the second Trump administration, when sweeping executive orders were deployed in rapid succession, their goal was to overwhelm the public and press with chaos. Immigration bans. Climate rollbacks. LGBTQ+ protections stripped. DEI programs defunded. Each announcement distracted from the next, creating a churn of outrage too fast to metabolize and too frequent to resist. The tactic wasn't new, but it was effective: Keep the public exhausted, reactive, and fragmented, making it easier to pass harmful policies that create widespread control.

Meanwhile, essential public services—the very systems that support human well-being—were quietly gutted. Government-funded mental health programs faced deep budget cuts. Suicide prevention and crisis hotlines, including 988 resources, suffered reduced staffing and limited reach. Schools and community health centers lost access to grants meant to provide trauma-informed care. A direct deprioritization of care, connection, and collective safety.

This isn't about partisanship. It's about empathy, or the lack thereof, as a governing principle. When leadership is driven by division rather than care, by dominance rather than service, our social fabric frays. And the people most impacted—queer youth, disabled communities, immigrants, survivors of violence—are told, implicitly or explicitly, that their suffering is a price worth paying for someone else's comfort.

In a disconnected society, it's not hard to sell scapegoats. But in a connected one, it's much harder to look a neighbor in the eye and justify their dehumanization. And yet, here's the tension I keep circling back to: The people reading this book, *you*, probably aren't the ones who need it most. If you're here, it likely means you already value empathy. You've already begun to question the systems around you, to challenge inherited beliefs, to soften where the world has hardened you. But I'd be lying if I said I wrote this only for you. I wrote it with others in mind, too. The sorority sister who fell down the rabbit hole of conspiracy videos. The relative parroting rhetoric that turns human beings into caricatures. The friend whose fear and disillusionment made them susceptible to authoritarianism disguised as nationalism.

That's what disconnection does—it blinds people to the harm they're causing. It numbs them to suffering that isn't their own. And sometimes, it turns them into foot soldiers for cruelty masquerading as conviction.

I hope this book lands in their hands. I hope they sit with these stories, these studies, these truths, and feel something shift. But if this book can't reach them, maybe you can. Maybe your conversations will ripple out. Maybe your presence will soften something. Maybe your empathy, even when it's not returned, can be the first crack in someone's armor.

Reimagining What Action Looks Like

When people think of action, they often picture megaphones and marches. Petitions. Protests. Public platforms. And while those can be vital expressions of empathy in motion, they're not the only way to participate in change. Not everyone is called to organize, and not every meaningful act happens in public.

I've never participated in a public protest—not because I don't care, but because I feel called to engage differently. My activism doesn't show up in crowds; it surfaces in conversation. I've confronted relatives across dinner tables and challenged strangers in one-on-one moments when silence felt like complicity. I speak up when I see someone being mistreated, and I make it clear when a line has been crossed. For me, action is intimate. It's direct. And it matters just as much as marching.

Action isn't always dramatic. Often, it's layered into the invisible rhythms of our lives—how we spend our money, whose stories we center, what we teach, reward, tolerate, and challenge. It's how we behave in the spaces where no one is watching.

Empathy-driven action starts with a simple reframe: that your daily decisions aren't separate from the world's trajectory; they're part of it. The way you show up at work, in your community, online, and at home creates ripple effects. Small, consistent choices add up. Research in behavioral science shows that social norms—the invisible rules about what's acceptable or expected—can shift rapidly when enough individuals model a new way of being. This is called dynamic norm theory, and it suggests that when people believe others are beginning to change, they're more likely to change, too (Sparkman & Walton, 2017). So while your choice to speak up or extend care might feel insignificant, it's often the spark that makes others feel safe to do the same.

We also need to reimagine action as relational, not just individual. A single act of kindness matters, but so does your role in shaping environments that foster collective care. This means supporting policies that promote mental health access, education equity, and community resilience. It means shifting culture, not just hearts.

If empathy is to thrive in the long run, it must be reinforced structurally. We can't rely on individuals to carry the full weight of change in a system that rewards self-preservation over solidarity. But when people begin to act together, the ground starts to shift.

How to Become a Catalyst for Change

Change doesn't require a title. It doesn't wait for credentials or a perfect plan. It begins with people—ordinary people—choosing to live differently in a world that keeps telling them not to care. Becoming a catalyst for change isn't about being the loudest in the room; it's about consistency. Integrity. Deciding that the way you move through the world—how you speak, show up, and relate—can be a vehicle for collective healing.

The science supports this. Habit formation, once thought to be purely personal, is also profoundly social. Studies on behavioral contagion show that emotions, attitudes, and behaviors spread through networks like ripples in water. When you act with empathy, it doesn't stop with you—it influences those around you, who, in turn, influence others (Christakis & Fowler, 2009). Change travels person to person. Moment to moment. It's less like a lightning strike and more like a slow, steady fire that catches.

Empathy becomes sustainable when it's integrated—not treated like a grand gesture, but folded into your routines. That's how it becomes part of your identity. Behavioral scientists call this identity-based habit formation, a process in which repeated actions shape how you see yourself and, in turn, reinforce your behavior (Clear, 2018). When you begin to think, *I'm someone who speaks up*, *I'm someone who listens deeply*, or *I'm someone who creates safe spaces*, those choices become easier to maintain. They become who you are.

And if that identity feels too far from where you are now, remember: You don't have to make the leap all at once. You just have to take the next right step. One action. One shift in response. One decision to stay open when it would be easier to shut down. That's how movements begin—not always in the streets, but in the nervous system. In the rewiring of our instincts. More importantly, in the slow undoing of fear.

Becoming a catalyst also means learning how to hold the tension between urgency and grace. Yes, we are running out of time. Yes, the world is burning—both figuratively and literally. But we don't transform by sprinting alone. We transform by modeling a new pace. A new posture. A new paradigm for what it means to be human with each other.

So ask yourself: What do you want to stand for when things feel unstable? What does care look like in your corner of the world? What would shift if you treated every encounter like an opportunity to return someone to themselves? You may never see the full impact of your choices, but you don't need to. What matters is that you become the kind of person who plants seeds anyway—especially when the soil is dry, or when others have stopped believing things can grow.

You're not here to save the world. You're here to remind it what it feels like to be seen. Empathy, on its own, won't change the world, either. But empathy in motion? That just might. Empathy doesn't live in theory. It lives in people. In stories. In the moments where we choose connection over coincidence, care over comfort, and understanding over ego.

Jack taught me this in the middle of an airport terminal. No fanfare, no audience. Just a moment of chaos—delayed flights, panicked families, overwhelmed staff—and his calm, proactive presence. He stepped in without being asked, helping a total stranger navigate the mess so she didn't feel so alone.

Maren, thousands of miles away at the bottom of the world, offered a different kind of wisdom. She brought a grounded presence to an otherwise fast and adventure-filled trip. Maren taught me that mindfulness is more than meditation—it's relational. It's how we anchor ourselves to each other.

Matteo brought joy back into the equation. Through dance, he modeled what openness looks like in action. He broke down barriers not with debate, but with an open hand and a warm smile. Matteo's willingness to engage created space for me to do the same.

River and Lucy offered a more layered lens into community. River's home was warm, open, lived-in—a place where people felt safe to show up as they were. Lucy, on the other hand, chased perfection through anxious hospitality, trying to earn connection through control. Together, they represent the duality of how environments impact our nervous system, and how intention isn't enough without regulation.

Brandon had to unlearn everything. Once stuck in abusive cycles he couldn't name, he eventually recreated those same cycles in his love life, until he decided life wasn't worth living anymore. His story reminds us that environments—both physical and emotional—shape our sense of worth. Just as toxic spaces reinforce harm, nurturing ones rebuild us. Healing isn't about erasing the past, but about choosing what to carry forward.

Sam brought depth to every conversation we had. Her reflections on love, loss, identity, and longing weren't always easy, but they were honest. She questioned norms others accepted. She made space for paradox. Her story invited a reimagining of what life could look like when we stop performing and start reflecting. Sam didn't just live deeply—she invited others to do the same. And in a culture obsessed with the surface, that kind of depth is radical.

And finally, there's Dr. Abrams, who modeled resistance in its most liberating form. When I told him I was considering a Ph.D., he looked me in the eye and asked, "Do you want the title, or the life?" He wasn't dismissing education; he was critiquing the system. His resistance wasn't loud, but it was deliberate. He helped me see that choosing joy, curiosity, and authenticity is resistance in a culture that worships productivity and prestige. And that empathy, when applied inward, becomes clarity. If it weren't for Dr. Abrams, you probably wouldn't be reading this book—I likely would have been pulled in a different direction, pursuing research sponsored by a faculty member in an area I'm not super enthusiastic about. Instead, I'm writing the sociopolitical version of Dr. Bessel van der Kolk's *The Body Keeps the Score.*

Together, these stories form a mosaic. None of them "fixed" the world. But each, in their own way, changed it—by showing up, softening, staying open, and choosing care when disconnection would have been easier. This is how change happens. One choice, one moment, one person at a time.

I hope it starts with you.

Conclusion

If there's one truth woven through every story in these pages, it's that connection doesn't just *happen*. It's something we create, moment by moment, in the smallest of ways. And every small moment matters—a lot more than we often let ourselves believe.

We live in a time that rewards speed, certainty, and self-preservation. That kind of world will always try to convince you that care is optional, empathy is earned, and safety is something you have to secure for yourself before you can offer it to anyone else. But the stories you've read—from strangers in airports to friends on dance floors, from quiet leaders in Antarctica to communities rallying after disaster—prove otherwise.

Care doesn't require a grand gesture. It occurs naturally through presence. It shines in the courage to stay open when it would be easier to close. It acknowledges safety as a shared state and that your calm, attuned presence might be the very thing that helps someone else's nervous system finally settle.

Empathy won't always be convenient. You will feel the pull toward distraction, the instinct to protect your own energy, the fatigue of a world that asks for too much and gives too little in return. Offer care anyway. Choose connection. Not because it's easy, but because it's what makes us human.

Every one of us has the ability to narrow the space between loneliness and belonging—to make the choice, again and again, to see someone, to listen, to soften, to reach across what divides us. Those choices ripple outward in ways we'll never be able to measure, and they change the texture of the world we share.

The empathy deficit will not close because of one sweeping policy or one charismatic leader. It will close because ordinary people, people like you and me, decide that kindness will not be a transaction. When we commit to the understanding that presence is not an afterthought, we're able to show up for one another, even when the world tells us not to.

So, let this be your invitation: Notice the moment. Extend your hand. Offer to help someone. Ask the question that allows them to feel understood. Do it without keeping score. And when you feel the weight of the world on your shoulders, let someone else carry part of it with you.

Because in the end, it's not just connection that keeps us alive—it's the care we're willing to give and receive without condition. That's how we rebuild trust and repair what's broken. That's how we remember what it means to be human.

To the pillars of this story—my story—whose presence, courage, and care have been both compass and anchor along the way:

To Jack, who reminded me that the purest acts of care are given freely, without ledger or expectation, and that sometimes the smallest act of kindness can shift the ground beneath someone's feet. May you continue to ripple outward—slowly, softly, powerfully.

To Maren, who taught me to slow down enough to experience my life in real-time, to let go of the need to hold on, and to trust that the present moment will hold me if I simply let it. I hope the world continues to offer you moments worth lingering in and the quiet space to feel them fully.

To Matteo, who extended his hand and reminded me that courage doesn't always roar—it often begins quietly, in the choice to take up space when it would be easier to stay small. May you always find yourself dancing in rooms that your spirit radiates in.

To River, whose open door and steady warmth proved that safety is not built from walls or decor, but from the unspoken permission to breathe freely in another's presence. I hope your home, in all its forms, will always be a refuge for both yourself and for others.

To Lucy, who, without meaning to, showed me that tension can dress itself as hospitality, and that sometimes what we need most is less perfection, and more ease. May your loved ones always cherish you and give you space to land.

To Brandon, whose presence, however brief, reminded me that change often starts with a single decision to show up differently than the world expects of you. May you rest in peace and honor in your memory.

To Sam, who challenged the systems that asked for blind trust, and in doing so, gave countless others permission to question, to imagine, and to choose differently. I hope your courage is always met with the change you seek.

To Dr. Abrams, who offered one sentence that rerouted my entire life trajectory, proving that words, when timed and spoken with care, can become turning points. May your words continue to open doors for those still searching for their way through.

And to you, dear reader—you've walked beside me through these stories, carrying pieces of them now in your own hands. I hope they take root in the quiet spaces of your life, blooming when you least expect them.

This story isn't mine anymore; it's ours. And the way we choose to live it—together—will decide what comes next.

Acknowledgements

This book would not exist without the people who have shaped me, challenged me, and stood beside me through every chapter of my life. These pages carry pieces of their love, their wisdom, and their patience. To my parents, for always riding the waves in our relationship and never giving up on "us." When I first told my parents I was going back to school to become a therapist, my dad—who was not particularly known to swear—replied, "Oh, fuck." Dad, I hope I've made you proud (and a little less scared). To my editors at Finesse Books, for letting this book become what it was always meant to be, for trusting me to write it at my own pace, and for believing I'd get it done. To Dr. A at NYU, for reminding me that I can create social impact and achieve everything I've ever dreamed of without bending to the rigidity of academia. To Kelly McKenna, my first business coach and a pillar in building my platform on Instagram, thank you for always cheering me on and holding the vision with me after all these years. To my community in New York City—to Jules, Fred, Bailey, Katie, Erick, Alex, and Holly, both old friends and new—for teaching me the value of care, connection, and showing up for one another. To Jess, whose unwavering support reaches me in the form of voice notes from across the globe, for growing with me through every chapter and always guiding me towards self-reflection. To Eric, who, when I texted him asking if he would prefer to be named Ethan or Eli in this book, replied, "Can't I just be Eric?" Thank you for always being you, for asking the hard questions, for trying to understand where I'm coming from despite our radically different beliefs, and for being one of my oldest and very best friends.

And last, but certainly not least, to my therapist, Kate—whose guidance turned my pain into possibility—for holding space for my mess and my becoming, for walking with me through some of the hardest chapters, and for helping me write new ones. I wouldn't be here today if it weren't for you.

References

AQI. (2024, February 2). Finland & PISA: A fall from grace – but still a high performer. AQI. https://www.aqi.org.uk/blog s/finland-pisa-a-fall-from-grace-but-still-a-high-performer/

Arendt, H. (1963). Eichmann in Jerusalem: A report on the banality of evil. Viking Press.

Buchanan, L., Bui, Q., & Patel, J. K. (2020, July 3). Black Lives Matter may be the largest movement in U.S. history. The New York Times. https://www.nytimes.com/interactive/202 0/07/03/us/george-floyd-protests-crowd-size.html

Carson, J., Carson, K., Gil, K. M., & Baucom, D. H. (2004). Mindfulness-based relationship enhancement. Behavior Therapy, 35, 471–494. https://doi.org/10.1016/S0005-78 94(04)80028-5

Christakis, N. A., & Fowler, J. H. (2009). Connected: The surprising power of our social networks and how they shape our lives. Little, Brown and Company.

Clear, J. (2018). Atomic habits: An easy & proven way to build good habits & break bad ones. Avery.

Costa, P. T., Jr., & McCrae, R. R. (1992). Revised NEO personality inventory and NEO five-factor inventory professional manual. Odessa, FL: Psychological Assessment Resources.

Durkheim, É. (1912). The elementary forms of religious life (K. E. Fields, Trans.). Free Press. (Original work published 1912)

Esses, V. M., Medianu, S., & Lawson, A. (2013). Uncertainty, threat, and the role of the media in promoting the dehumanization of immigrants and refugees. Journal of Social Issues, 69. https://doi.org/10.1111/josi.12027

Federal Bureau of Investigation. (2024). 2023 Hate Crime Statistics. https://cde.ucr.cjis.gov/LATEST/webapp/#/pages/explorer/crime/hate-crime

Freyd, J. J. (1996). Betrayal trauma: The logic of forgetting childhood abuse. Harvard University Press.

Freyd, J. J. (2008). Betrayal trauma. In G. Reyes, J. D. Elhai, & J. D. Ford (Eds.), Encyclopedia of Psychological Trauma (pp. 76–78). John Wiley & Sons.

Gabriel, S., Valenti, J., & Young, A. F. (2017). Collective effervescence: The emotional experience of collective gatherings. Journal of Positive Psychology, 12(5), 468–480. https://doi.org/10.1037/pas0000434

Gallup. (2023, May 2). Quarter of Americans report feeling very or fairly lonely. https://news.gallup.com/opinion/gallup/512618/almost-quarter-world-feels-lonely.aspx

Hamilton, W. D. (1964). The genetical evolution of social behaviour. Journal of Theoretical Biology, 7(1), 1–16. https://doi.org/10.1016/0022-5193(64)90038-4

Hamlin, J. K., Wynn, K., & Bloom, P. (2007). Social evaluation by preverbal infants. Nature, 450(7169), 557–559. https://doi.org/10.1038/nature06288

Hare, R. D. (1999). Without conscience: The disturbing world of the psychopaths among us. Guilford Press.

Kabat-Zinn, J. (2003). Mindfulness-based interventions in context: Past, present, and future. Clinical Psychology: Science and Practice, 10(2), 144–156. https://doi.org/10.1093/clipsy.bpg016

Lorenz, E. N. (1972). Predictability: Does the flap of a butterfly's wings in Brazil set off a tornado in Texas? American Association for the Advancement of Science.

Luks, A., & Payne, P. (1992). The healing power of doing good: the health and spiritual benefits of helping others. Fawcett Columbine.

Merriam-Webster. (n.d.). Progressivism. In Merriam-Webster.com dictionary. Retrieved May 11, 2025, from https://www.merriam-webster.com/dictionary/progressivism

Pew Research Center. (2022, August 9). Americans' political divisions persist, but fewer say differences are due to party affiliation. https://www.pewresearch.org/wp-content/uploads/sites/20/2022/08/PP_2022.09.08_partisan-hostility_REPORT.pdf

Pew Research Center. (2023). Religion in America: U.S. Religious Landscape Study. Pew Research Center. https://www.pewresearch.org/religious-landscape-study/

Porges, S. W. (2004). Neuroception: A subconscious system for detecting threats and safety. Zero to Three, 24(5), 19–24.

Post, S. G. (2005). Altruism, Happiness, and Health: It's Good to Be Good. International Journal of Behavioral Medicine, 12(2), 66–77. https://doi.org/10.1207/s15327558ijbm1202_

Rizzolatti, G., Fadiga, L., Gallese, V., & Fogassi, L. (1996). Premotor cortex and the recognition of motor actions. Cognitive Brain Research, 3(2), 131–141. https://doi.org/10.1016/0926-6410(95)00038-0

Sparkman, G., & Walton, G. M. (2017). Dynamic norms promote sustainable behavior, even if it is unpopular. Psychological Science, 28(11), 1663–1674. https://doi.org/10.1177/0956797617719950

Tang, Y. Y., Hölzel, B. K., & Posner, M. I. (2015). The neuroscience of mindfulness meditation. Nature Reviews Neuroscience, 16(4), 213–225. https://doi.org/10.1038/nrn3916

The Trevor Project. (2024). 2024 National Survey on LGBTQ+ Youth Mental Health. https://www.thetrevorproject.org/survey-2024/

Trivers, R. L. (1971). The evolution of reciprocal altruism. Quarterly Review of Biology, 46(1), 35–57. https://doi.org/1 0.1086/406755

Turner, J. C., Brown, R. J., & Tajfel, H. (1979). Social comparison and group interest in ingroup favouritism. European Journal of Social Psychology, 9(2), 187–204. https://doi .org/10.1002/ejsp.2420090207

U.S. Department of Health and Human Services. (2023). Our epidemic of loneliness and isolation: The U.S. Surgeon General's Advisory on the Healing Effects of Social Connection and Community. https://www.hhs.gov/sites/default/files/sur geon-general-social-connection-advisory.pdf

www.ingramcontent.com/pod-product-compliance
Lightning Source LLC
Chambersburg PA
CBHW031126020426
42333CB00012B/253